Pronouncing Shakespeare: The Globe Experiment

How did Shakespeare's plays sound when they were originally performed? How can we know, and could the original pronunciation ever be recreated? For three days in June 2004 Shakespeare's Globe presented their production of *Romeo and Juliet* in original, Shakespearian pronunciation. This book tells the story of how it happened . . .

In an unusual blend of autobiography, narrative, and academic content, reflecting the unique nature of the experience, David Crystal recounts the first attempt in over fifty years to mount a full-length Shakespeare play in original pronunciation. The story begins by introducing the Globe theatre and its approach to 'original practices', which had dealt with all aspects of Elizabethan stagecraft – except pronunciation. It traces the way the idea developed, from the initial proposal in 2003 through planning and rehearsals to the full-scale production in 2004. A large section is devoted to the nature of the Early Modern English sound system and the evidence for it. Other major sections include reports of how the actors coped with the task of learning the pronunciation, how it affected their performances, and how the audiences reacted.

DAVID CRYSTAL is one of the world's foremost authorities on language. He is author of the hugely successful *Cambridge Encyclopedia of Language* (1987; second edition 1997), *Cambridge Encyclopedia of the English Language* (1995; second edition 2003), and *English as a Global Language* (1997; second edition 2003). An internationally renowned writer, journal editor, lecturer, and broadcaster, he received an OBE in 1995 for his services to the study and teaching of the English language. His previous work on Shakespeare includes two books written with his actor son, Ben, *Shakespeare's Words* (2002) and *The Shakespeare Miscellany* (2005).

Pronouncing Shakespeare: The Globe Experiment

DAVID CRYSTAL

CAMBRIDGE UNIVERSITY PRESS
Cambridge, New York, Melbourne, Madrid, Cape Town, Singapore, São Paulo

Cambridge University Press
The Edinburgh Building, Cambridge, CB2 2RU, UK
Published in the United States of America by Cambridge University Press, New York

www.cambridge.org
Information on this title: www.cambridge.org/9780521852135

First published 2005

Printed in the United Kingdom at the University Press, Cambridge

A catalogue record for this book is available from the British Library

ISBN-13 978-0-521-85213-5 hardback
ISBN-10 0-521-85213-7 hardback

Cambridge University Press has no responsibility for the persistence or accuracy of
URLs for external or third-party internet websites referred to in this book, and does not
guarantee that any content on such websites is, or will remain, accurate or appropriate.

To all at Shakespeare's Globe

For three days in June 2004, Shakespeare's Globe presented their production of *Romeo and Juliet* in original, Shakespearian pronunciation. This book tells the story of how it happened.

CONTENTS

Preface   xi

Prologue by Tim Carroll   xv

1   Idea   1

2   Proposal   11

3   Evidence   43

4   Rehearsal   97

5   Performance   133

6   Consequences   161

Epilogue   173

Appendix 1   Chief distinctive Early Modern English
             vowels   175

Appendix 2   Extracts from the transcription   177

Appendix 3   Audio-visual aids   181

Index   183

PREFACE

This has been a curious book to write – an unusual blend of biography, narrative, and academic content. It reflects the unusual nature of the experience. It cannot be often that academic linguists find themselves so intimately involved in the theatre world, or for theatre practitioners to be so heavily involved with historical linguistics. But the integration of the two domains is exciting, in whichever direction one travels.

The person who made this journey first, in living memory, was John Barton, who approached it from the opposite direction. If this book were being dedicated to any one person, it would have to be him, for his production of a Shakespeare play in Elizabethan pronunciation took place in 1952, when I was eleven and had yet to see my first Shakespeare play (Paul Robeson's *Othello*, seven years later – in which, incidentally, Sam Wanamaker played Iago).

When I met Barton, while preparing this book, his first words to me were: 'You are a lucky fellow.' I knew it. In my non-linguistic life I have had a lifetime amateur or semi-professional relationship with the theatre. I have acted in several repertory companies, as has my wife, directed a few times, and toured my own shows. We have a son who became a professional actor. For years we have spent an annual holiday in Stratford. So it is easy to imagine that, for me, there could be no more entrancing world outside linguistic walls than this one; and to be involved in it, for a few months, was fortune indeed.

It was, in many ways, the project of a lifetime – a real voyage of exploration, for all concerned. All praise to the Globe, I say, for committing themselves to it. And my thanks to the prime movers there, for asking me to be part of it.

The book had to be written quickly, while the performances were fresh in my mind – and in the minds of those who participated. I am most grateful to everyone at the theatre for their help in making all the arrangements which enabled me to be in the right place at the right time, and to talk to everyone involved, both directly and virtually.

David Crystal

Holyhead, July 2004

PROLOGUE

Tim Carroll

Almost everything about this project was last minute. The decision to go ahead, all decisions about *how* to go ahead, even the appointment of a dialect coach – they all happened long after they should have done, if we were to do the thing properly. The reasons for this are boringly easy to imagine (money, scheduling problems, my own lack of organization); what is not so easy to explain is why it ended up working so well.

Over the last few years that I have worked at the Globe, I have spent a lot of time thinking about the nature of Shakespeare's language. I have always been very interested in what, if anything, Shakespeare's use of verse implies about the way the plays should be spoken. In particular, I have often noticed that an actor can create quite a pleasing effect by picking out those phrases (not so rare) which are still in use today and speaking them in as modern and 'street' a way as possible – 'What do you mean?' 'How do I look?'. I have often felt that this short-term success came at a long-term cost: that it is a bit like performing a play in French, except that every time you come across a word like *association* that is the same as the English word, you pronounce it in English. This might help understanding fractionally, but it would destroy any chance of our believing we are listening to a language that anyone ever spoke. I have long felt that a strict attention to the metre might well create a language that, even if it took a little getting used to, would sound unified, and therefore more lifelike.

The three performances of *Romeo and Juliet* in original pronunciation gave me a glimpse of that longed-for event. Imperfect as it was, it was nonetheless possible to hear that real people were talking to each other. To be sure, some previously well-known words were less familiar, but in that they were in the same boat as the characters in their original-practice costumes: we might not recognize them, we might not understand or even like them, but we can see that they belong together, that they come from one world. Out here, in the yard, in the galleries, in the chimney of Tate Modern – all around us – is another world. And what an extraordinary place it is where these two worlds can meet.

Not everything about this project was last minute. One element that pre-dated this summer was my desire to hear a Shakespeare play sound as it might have done 400 years ago. That desire has been with me for a long time, and for its realization I am eternally grateful to Mark Rylance, who gave the project the green light; to Sid Charlton, Rowan Walker-Brown, Debs Callan, and everyone in the Theatre and Education Departments who worked to make it happen; to Tom Cornford for doing much of the heavy lifting; to Charmian Hoare for her wonderfully patient and skilful work with the actors; and of course to the author of this book. What the following account will not tell you, but you will easily work out for yourself, is that the main reason this project did not end up in disaster is David Crystal. Had he done as many of us would have done, and brought an air of arrogant omniscience to the rehearsal room, the whole thing could have been scuppered from the start. But instead, from the very beginning, he insisted on being clear about what he knew and what he didn't. In so doing he set an example of humble enquiry that liberated the rest of us. Suddenly we were reminded of what it is so easy to forget: that the heart of the enterprise is not display but discovery.

CHAPTER 1

Idea

Do you know the Globe? Shakespeare's reconstructed Globe theatre, on the south bank of the Thames, nestling between London Bridge and the Tate Modern. Look at it from the river, and at first sight it seems totally out of place, with the multi-laned city traffic to the left and the towering chimney of the renovated gallery to the right. But look from the south bank in the direction of St Paul's, and try to think back in time a little, and suddenly it is the twentieth-century traffic and chimney which are out of place. The Globe seems as if it might have been there for centuries.

And in a sense it was. For the first Globe was built in 1599 very close to where the current building stands. We know this because there are several printed panoramic views of London, dating from around 1600, which show the theatre among the buildings of Southwark. The original site is now largely buried under the foundations of modern apartments, 200 yards away, but what is 200 yards when you are trying to achieve a vision? And that is what the reconstructed Globe is – a vision.

The vision belonged to American actor, director, and producer Sam Wanamaker, who conceived the project after his first visit to London, as long ago as 1949. In 1970 he formed the Globe Playhouse Trust dedicated to the reconstruction of the theatre and the provision of education and exhibition facilities. A huge amount of fundraising later, the site was bought and the building completed. The Globe mounted its first production, *The Two Gentlemen of Verona*, in a 'prologue season' towards the end of summer 1996. It took place on a temporary stage, with much of the outside area still a building site. Then, in May 1997, the official opening took place, with the company performing four plays by Elizabethan dramatists, including two by Shakespeare. Sadly, Sam Wanamaker saw none of this. He had died from cancer in December 1993.

The reconstruction is as close to the original as modern scholars and traditional craftworkers can make it. Excavations on the sixteenth-century site in 1990 indicated that it was a twenty-sided building with a diameter of 100 feet – fitting the description (with a little poetic licence) of the 'wooden O' referred to by the Chorus in *Henry V*. We know that timbers from the demolished Theatre playhouse in Shoreditch were carried across the Thames by members of the company to help build it. There are hints about its interior in contemporary accounts, both from the builders and from those who attended plays there. A contemporary sketch of another Elizabethan theatre, the Swan, suggests a possible stage layout, but the design of the Globe stage, and especially the location of the two large pillars holding up the roof, was a matter of considerable conjecture.

The project used building techniques which replicated, as far as possible, those used at the time. Green oak was cut and shaped according to sixteenth-century practice. Lime plaster was mixed following a contemporary recipe. Water-reed thatch was used for the roof, based on samples found during the excavation. Each element of the balustrades was turned by hand by woodworkers. The demands of

modern fire precautions of course placed limits on
what could be done, and such things as illuminated
fire-exit signs, two additional exits, and extra lighting
were introduced to meet the safety needs of a modern
audience, as well as to aid visibility during evening
performances. It is possible to hire a cushion to
reduce the impact of the wooden benches on sensitive modern posteriors. There are toilets on site. And
when it rains, the groundlings in the yard, open to
the elements, can buy plastic capes. But apart from
these nods in the direction of modern comfort and
convenience, the building gives its visitors a powerful
impression of authenticity. It feels right, even though
scholarly debate continues.

Or, at least, it feels like nothing else in the modern
theatrical world. The Globe, despite its contradic-
tions (such as Elizabethan dress on stage; modern
dress in the audience), has presented a challenge to
modern theatrical values. The journey has been
a process of exploration, a voyage of discovery.
Would a modern theatre audience be prepared to
stand for three hours to watch a play? Would they
interact with the actors, when invited to do so?

Would they interact when *not* so invited, and what would the actors do then? How can one turn a fixed structure, with all its performance limitations, the result of highly informed guesswork – but guesswork nonetheless – to best advantage? There has been plenty of opposition, as well as support, for the Globe project. The principle has been to introduce radical ideas tempered with caution, to look for ways of liberating performance without doing things that get in the way.

One of the most interesting outcomes has been to draw attention to the process of dramatic interactivity, demonstrating the creative role of the playgoer. My most vivid memories of productions are those where that mysterious border between actor and spectator is crossed. And it is language that usually provides the bridge. I had never thought of Caliban as a hero until I heard the entire audience, football-crowd-like, shouting 'Ban, ban, Ca-caliban' over and over in support for him as we approached the interval in the 2000 production of *The Tempest*. I had never achieved a full sense of the patriotic fervour implicit in *Henry V* until I heard (in 1997) the entire audience, pantomime-like, shouting support for the English side against the French – or at least, most of us, for a group of French tourists in the audience vociferously shouted in the other direction, much to the delight of the French nobles. I had never expected to be placed on the spot by Hamlet, until I found myself responding aloud, along with everyone else, to Mark Rylance's full-frontal question, 'Am I a coward?', in the 2000 production. Whether the effects were stage-managed or spontaneous, each regular Globegoer will have a personal audio-visual picture album of actor–audience memories to match mine.

The open-air venue adds its own character to the occasion. It is not just a matter of the sun, wind, and rain making their contribution. Birds fly in and out. Performances and performers have to contend with the noise of London – police sirens, helicopters, air-busses en route to Heathrow ... During one perform-ance in the *Romeo and Juliet* weekend, the actors fought for half an hour against two helicopters cir-cling overhead, as the Olympic torch arrived nearby. During another, there was a torrential downpour, and a lightning accompaniment which might have suited King Lear but did not gain the approval of the Nurse. Often the interventions work to advantage. 'The isle is full of noises', said Caliban, at one of the *Tempest* performances – and to everyone's delight, a pair of river-boats hooted. And at one point in Juliet's anguished speech about Romeo being banished, a nonchalant pigeon landed on the stage in front of her, but quickly lost its nonchalance when Juliet went for it.

Nobody at the Globe much likes the word 'authentic'. It is a difficult adjective to justify, given that so little is known about theatrical practice in Shakespeare's time, and the modern environment inevitably makes its presence felt, as does the modern weather. Performances take place for only half the year, between May and September. Evening performances are routine, whereas they were afternoons-only, at the original Globe. The theatre itself can be no more than a 'best guess' as to how things were. And the same sense of limitation pervades all aspects of the productions – casting, clothing, properties, design, music, movement … Every attempt at an 'original practice' is an experiment, whether it be the casting of men in women's roles, the design and making of contemporary costume, or the performance of songs and instrumental music. The Globe has nonetheless carved out for itself an enviable reputation in each of these areas. Although by no means restricting itself to original practices – for example, there have been productions in modern dress, as well as all-female casts – it is, to my mind, what it does best. And, throughout its first twenty-eight productions, from 1996 to 2003, its audiences have been exposed to interpretations of most aspects of the Elizabethan stage. With one striking exception. The Globe had not touched original pronunciation (OP).

Tim Carroll, the *Romeo and Juliet* Master of Play, had thought of doing a production in OP before, when the company was planning *Twelfth Night* in 2002. He had even suggested that it might be used for the whole run. Nobody doubted the spirit of the argument – that original practice in pronunciation was just as valid an aim as original practice in any other area of stagecraft. But in-house opinion was, understandably, against it. The chief problem was that nobody knew just how it would sound. Perhaps it would be so different from present-day pronunciation that audiences would simply not be able to follow it? An unintelligible play could produce an attendance catastrophe. No theatre, least of all the Globe, with its attendances restricted to five months of the year, and just four plays in production, could afford to alienate a quarter of its audience. They dropped the idea.

But, like all good ideas, the thought would not go away. Tim kept getting asked, in workshops, 'How did it sound originally?', and found himself unable to answer the question. So, in the planning for the 2004 season, he returned to it. This time he suggested a three-performance experiment, a month into the season. It would be publicized as such, so that audiences would know they would be getting something different. There was still some in-house uncertainty. Would the actors be able to cope with two versions of the play to perform? Would it not require two rehearsal regimes, in a very tight schedule? Tim had another argument. Surely the Globe had to be the first to mount such a production, in modern times?

There had been no such experiment since John Barton's *Julius Caesar* in 1952. If the Globe didn't do it, someone else would. Could the Globe live with that? The answer was no. Artistic director Mark Rylance gave the experiment his blessing. And so it was decided, in the autumn of 2003, that for the Globe's twenty-ninth production the resonances of Elizabethan English would once again be heard on a stage in Southwark.

CHAPTER 2

Proposal

At the time, I knew none of this. The first inkling I had that something was in the offing was an email in December from Debs Callan, Head of Continuing Education. The message mentioned that the Globe was planning an OP weekend for the last weekend in June, and that Globe Education wanted to support and help inform the work of the Theatre Department by setting up a study weekend ahead of the performances, at the beginning of that month. The aim was to provide a forum for discussion between theatre practitioners and scholars about the nature of Elizabethan pronunciation. What did I think?

I wasn't surprised to get such a message. My links with the Globe had become steadily stronger since 1997, when Nick Robins, the editor of the membership magazine *Around the Globe*, had asked me to write a regular piece on Shakespeare's neologisms – or

Williamisms, as I went on to call them – for his magazine. As part of the Globe Education seasons, I had presented a few performance lectures on Shakespeare's language – a mixture of academic commentary and theatrical presentation, supported by actor son Ben. In 2003 I had the privilege of becoming the Sam Wanamaker Fellow for that year, and towards the end of the year I found myself working with Globe Education as a consultant for Wordplay, one of their schools outreach programmes. So I suppose I fell into the category of 'tame linguist', as far as the Globe was concerned. And no linguist could have been tamer and more ready to collaborate. I think the Globe is the most exciting theatrical project of modern times.

But the message made me think. It was a fine idea, but a difficult one to implement. In our book on Shakespeare's vocabulary, *Shakespeare's Words*, which had appeared in 2002, Ben and I had avoided representing Elizabethan pronunciation – or Early Modern English (EME), as it is more technically known – in all but a few very difficult cases (such as 'oeillade'). We felt most readers would have difficulty with a technical representation of the sounds – a phonetic transcription.

Would actors be any different? I remember Ben telling me that phonetic transcription was not routinely a part of actor training. It was not immediately obvious how to get round this problem.

And then, indeed, there was a great deal of uncertainty about EME pronunciation. Quite a lot of research has been done on how the vowels and consonants – the 'segments' of speech – were pronounced at the time, and on the rhythmical structure of words and lines, but there are many gaps in our knowledge. And it is impossible to reconstruct most aspects of the 'non-segmental' side of pronunciation – such features as intonation and tone of voice. We shall never know *exactly* what Hamlet meant by speaking 'trippingly upon the tongue' – though we can guess it was something to do with the speed and rhythm of colloquial speech. Previous attempts at OP had always been a mixture of old and new – old segments with a modern intonation superimposed. A new attempt could be no different.

As far as a seminar was concerned, I was anxious to point out to Debs what she was letting herself in for. Few readers of this book will ever have attended a conference of scholars who specialize in the history of pronunciation – historical phoneticians and phonologists. These people can spend many happy hours debating whether a vowel was pronounced a little bit further forward or further back in the mouth, and discussing which part of the tongue was involved in the production of a particular consonant. Such terms as 'debate' and 'discuss' underestimate the emotion of these occasions. Compared with historical phonology arguments, political rows in the House of Commons seem mild indeed.

It would not be easy, I felt, to obtain a meeting of minds between phoneticians, concerned with minute matters of articulation, and theatre people, concerned with general effects. It would be very important to define a clear set of aims for such a seminar. I was also puzzled – though I didn't mention this to Debs at the time – as to how a seminar provisionally scheduled for the beginning of June would actually help inform a production scheduled for the end of the same month. I did not know how long it would take actors to master the style of pronunciation, but they would surely have had to start rehearsals by then? There would be dramaturgical issues, which the director would want to address. The best role of a seminar, I thought, was one where scholars would combine their ideas as to what was known about EME pronunciation, so that the best possible transcription could be made. But that would require a seminar early in 2004 – well before rehearsals started, and allowing time to get the transcription written. It was probably out of the question. I doubted whether the specialists I knew who worked in this area would be able to attend a symposium called at such short notice. It would have to be at the beginning of January, before university term began. That was a fortnight away. I emailed a couple of colleagues, just to see. As I thought, no chance.

How, then, would the Globe get hold of a transcription? Perhaps they already had a version from someone. I had never heard of such a thing, and certainly not for this particular play, but what did I know? Maybe John Barton, or someone else who had investigated OP in the past, had been involved. So, as a bit of an afterthought, I added a last paragraph to my e-reply to Debs. 'If you want a transcription for the actors – if you haven't already got one – I could provide one at some point, I'm sure.' It was 12 December. Debs was going away. I got on with Christmas, and promptly forgot all about it.

Cut now to 16 January. Another email, this time from Tom Cornford, who introduced himself as Tim Carroll's assistant director. I was struck by the sentence which followed his greeting: 'I understand that you have offered to produce a phonetic version of the text for us for the original pronunciation performances.' I had? I checked my email. I had. Various Shakespearian phrases flashed across my mind – such as 'enterprises of great pith and moment'. And what was the bit again that followed 'O cursed spite...'?

Tom went on, in an apologetic barrage of questions. 'We are not sure where the issues of controversy are, and what the role of the symposium is. Is it going to be taking decisions which will affect your phonetic version? Are there particular elements of the job which you will be unable to do until the symposium has taken key decisions? Do you have a time-scale in mind for your version? Is there any research which we can help you with? And are there any decisions which you would like to take in consultation with us?' To which I thought, in Dogberrian reverse succession. Sixthly and fifthly, yes. Fourthly, no. Thirdly and secondly, don't know. And firstly, me neither.

I amplified. I made the points to Tom that I had thought of making to Debs, and copied her in. With a real issue to face, there was no way that text decisions could be left until the beginning of June. Either the seminar would have to be brought well forward, or it would have to change its character. It might even be better to have a seminar *after* the event – assuming that the performance was a success and there was a move to repeat the experiment. Whatever was decided, if I was to do a transcription I would have to get on with it promptly. I did some rapid calculations. This was mid-January. Rehearsals were to begin towards the end of March. First performance was 7 May. Assume the director and cast would not be spending time on the OP performances until, say, the end of May. So that would mean getting the transcription in by the beginning of May, or mid-May at the latest. Important to meet Tim Carroll and discuss how to proceed ASAP. Assume this meeting can't happen until end of January. That means just three months' preparation time. Twelve weeks to research it and present it. Could it be done?

I should explain. I already have a job. Several, in fact. Although I have been free-lance as an academic since 1985, each year I do some courses at the University of Wales in Bangor, where I am honorary professor, and in 2004 they were planned for – wouldn't you know? – February and March. I do a lot of lecturing at other venues, and am often abroad. I looked at my diary. Between February and the end of May I was scheduled for visits to Barcelona (twice), the Netherlands, and Stuttgart. Each week I had a lecture visit in Britain somewhere or other. And the other days I was expected in 'the office' – the place where my general encyclopedias get compiled and edited. During the first half of 2004 we were scheduled to produce a new edition of the Penguin *Factfinder*. The entire encyclopedia database was to be placed online by the beginning of March (it eventually surfaced as www.findout.tv). And the entire *Shakespeare's Words* database was scheduled to be online in time for Shakespeare's birthday, 23 April (that arrived, a few days late, as www.shakespeareswords.com). It was already a very busy year. Could it be done?

All of this reflection took, as I recall, some half a minute. And while I was reflecting, I realised that I had already made up my mind. It just had to be done.

Reaction

I began to get my thoughts in order. Could it be done, in the other sense? Was enough known to make a plausible stab at it? I turned to my library and pulled down the major works on EME. This would have to be an exercise in standing on shoulders. Fortunately, several powerful sets of shoulders were available. There was Helge Kökeritz's *Shakespeare's Pronunciation*, E. J. Dobson's *English Pronunciation 1500–1700*, and Charles Barber's *Early Modern English*. These were books from the 1950s, 1960s, and 1970s, respectively. There were extracts in transcription presented in such standard works as A. C. Gimson's *An Introduction to the Pronunciation of English*, which I had studied as a student. Several linguists, such as Roger Lass, had also specialized more recently in plotting pronunciation change through the period, and had written up their work in histories of the language, or in such publications as *The Cambridge History of the English Language*. There were disputes a-plenty and gaps in knowledge, but a great deal of unanimity too. I reckoned we could be about 80 per cent certain of how things were, as far as the vowels, consonants, and syllables were concerned. It was enough, I felt, on which to hazard a transcription of a whole play.

And in any case, I wasn't the first, by any means, to experiment with OP. As long ago as 1952, at Cambridge, John Barton had produced *Julius Caesar* in such a version for the Marlowe Society, and had maintained an interest in it ever since. He is well known in recent times for his readiness to produce some OP on request, and examples can be heard in the RSC's *Playing Shakespeare* series (1984) or in the BBC's *The Story of English* (1986). Others have shared his interest – Peter Hall, for example, who had been a member of Barton's cast. Tyrone Guthrie had worked with it at Stratford, Ontario. And I was aware that many Shakespearian scholars, actors, and enthusiasts had delved before me into Kökeritz and the others, in performances now lost to public memory. But nobody after Barton had gone for a full production, and there had never been one on a London stage. Barton himself had never repeated the experiment.

It is funny how things come together. Barton's linguistic source had been Professor Daniel Jones, the founding father of academic phonetics in Britain. Gimson was one of Daniel Jones's students. I was one of Gimson's. When I met John Barton in July 2004, and we compared our respective versions, I was not surprised to find them almost identical.

My reaction to Tom Cornford's email was a lengthy one, because a number of points had to be clarified. I was especially anxious that the directors should be aware of just what they were letting themselves in for, so that they could anticipate the effects of OP on their interpretation of the play. The bottom line was this: although EME pronunciation would not sound like any modern accent, it would undoubtedly suggest similarities with several regional accents of the present day. In particular – as we shall see in Chapter 3 – -*r* was sounded after vowels, in such words as *far* and *harm*, so that inevitably the accent would remind modern British listeners of rural speech, such as would be heard in the West Country, Ireland, and many other places. Other features of the accent would reinforce this impression, such as the centralized quality of some vowels and the dropping of the -*g* in such words as *running*. All characters would therefore end up sounding somewhat 'rustic', to modern ears. What effect would this have on the characterization, especially in maintaining a distinction between upper-class and lower-class characters? Can the older Capulets and Montagues, the Prince, and Romeo and Juliet themselves all sound rural without the effect becoming ludicrous?

I was especially worried that the actors might overdo it. This would only be natural. Something happens when people encounter a new accent or dialect and try to imitate it (either consciously or unconsciously). In the linguistics business it is called 'hypercorrection'. Newcomers notice the most distinctive features of the speech and use them more than the real speakers would. The result is a stereotype of the reality. We all do it. People who tell a Welsh joke say such things as 'look you, boyo', when no self-respecting Welsh person would ever say such a thing. Similarly, 'hoots mon', 'sure now begorrah', 'hern hern', 'ooh-aahr, Jim la-a-d', and other such distortions of (respectively, Scots, Irish, American, and West Country) dialect reality are commonplace in jocular expression. It was the last, mock-West-Country accent, which was at the back of my mind. There would be very little rehearsal time, and I didn't want the actors to be inadvertently slipping into a version of Robert Newton as Long John Silver.

This proved to be a real worry. Jumping ahead for a moment, several of the actors told me afterwards how they were concerned about slipping into just such a stereotype. Jimmy Garnon, who played Mercutio, summed it up:

Due to the number of vowel sounds in the OP that we recognize from regional accents around us today, it was incredibly easy to disappear down blind alleys. I found myself in Cork far more often than I should like, and at times felt I was just riffing along generalized Mummerset lines. The

difficulty, I suppose, being that without a solid, clear understanding in our mind of how we should sound, sounding
other in a non-specific way could deceive us into feeling
right. This was a worry in performance as I attempted to forget
entirely about the accent and concentrate on the character's
thoughts. Every now and then I'd feel a flash of panic and have
to listen to myself to check everything still felt in place. If off in
Cork, squirt a fat dose of Mummerset 'rrrr' in, and so on. I
know that coming off most scenes, Benvolio [Rhys Meredith]
and I instantly set about reassuring each other that we hadn't
just perpetrated a Pat and Mike double act!

They hadn't. And all of the actors managed to avoid
the trap.

They were probably much helped by a principle we
adopted very early on in the production: to let the
actors colour the OP by their own natural accent.
Some of the distinctive features of the accent could
be pronounced in several ways, then as now. Take
the -r which is heard after vowels, as in *hear* and *our*.
There are many ways in which this can be articulated
– as we can hear today in the different pronunciations of -r used by West Country, Scots, Welsh,
American, and South Asian speakers, for example.
You can hear the -r made at the front of the mouth,

with the tip of the tongue (the symbol in the International Phonetic Alphabet is [ɹ]), or at the back, with the uvula [ʁ]. You can hear it made with the tongue-tip very markedly curled back (so-called 'retroflex' r, [ʈ]). You can hear a single tap against the roof of the mouth [ɾ] or a lengthy trill [r]. You can hear a strong r-colouring or a very slight one. So, to say that in EME the -r was pronounced leaves open the question of exactly what kind of -r it was. If the actors had a natural accent which used one of these pronunciations, I saw no problem in allowing them to 'colour' their OP with that quality, if they wanted. And the same applied to the other distinctive features of the accent.

I did not want phonetic uniformity in the OP production. There would not have been such uniformity on the Elizabethan stage. London at the time was a melting-pot of accents (just as it is today), the population having just grown in size from around 50,000, at the beginning of the sixteenth century, to over 200,000 at the end. People were pouring into the capital from all over the country, but especially from East Anglia and the East Midlands. Three major dialect areas met in London – Southern, South-Eastern (Kentish), and East Midlands. Foreign accents were increasingly heard. There was an emerging notion of the 'best speech' being heard at Court, but this accent was changing its character with the times, and was nothing like the 'Received Pronunciation' (RP) associated with the royal family today. People such as Francis Drake and Walter Raleigh brought Devonshire accents to the Court. For some years after 1603, indeed, the court accent was Scottish, following the arrival of King James.

The actors on the Elizabethan stage came from many parts of the country, and would have brought their accents with them. Henry Condell was from Norwich. Robert Armin, Shakespeare's clown, was from Lynn in Norfolk. John Heminge was baptized in Worcestershire; he moved to London at age twelve, so would probably have rapidly accommodated to London speech. Shakespeare, moving there in his early twenties, would also have developed a mixed accent – Warwickshire–London, in his case. Whatever the exact character of these accents might have been, one thing is certain: they would not have been the same. All would have shared the core phonetic features of the 'accent of the age', but each would have been phonetically individual. We must remember that, in those days, there was no 'standard accent' to emulate – the accent we now know as RP (most often heard in the traditional voice of the BBC) did not emerge in England until the beginning of the nineteenth century. There was no drama-school system in Shakespearian times to teach actors how to enunciate. Diversity would have been the norm on the Elizabethan stage. So I had no compunction in suggesting that the Globe company retain its natural diversity, in approaching the OP production. And, in the event, that is what they did. I did not know it at the time, but my view reinforced Tim Carroll's, who would stress to his cast the importance of using their natural voices.

Back in mid-January, there was no way of predicting the accent range of the company. The casting was still taking place, and there was no focus on the OP production during auditions. So there was no guarantee that the cast would be a group of people who were good at accents – and I mean *really* good at accents. It is unfortunately all too common to hear accents on stage or film in which – notwithstanding the best efforts of dialect coaches – accuracy and consistency throughout the performance leaves, shall we say, a little to be desired. But at least in those situations, the actors have a contemporary model they can turn to for help. They can go to a part of the country and immerse themselves in the accent, if they want. Or listen to recordings. No such help here. Nobody had spoken the EME accent for the best part of 400 years. Jimmy Garnon expressed a general opinion: 'Learning it was trickier than any other accent I have encountered . . . it had no tune to grab hold of.'

The tune, of course, is the hardest thing to get across. Having worked with various transcriptions of the period, ever since student days, I could hear the tune of EME in my mind's ear. I had often used the published extracts in lectures on the history of English, sometimes reading aloud whole speeches from Shakespeare to give a class the auditory feel of the period. But how on earth could I get this across in accurate detail to a cry of players in a rehearsal period which would be less than a month? And for a whole play, not just a speech? And for such a diverse range of characters? The second half of my response to Tom Cornford's email, accordingly, focused on how this might be done.

Transcription

To transcribe or not to transcribe. That really was the question. I was not concerned about whether a plausible version of Shakespearian pronunciation could be reconstructed. I knew that could be done. The question I couldn't answer was how to write this pronunciation down on a page in such a way that it could be easily read and learned by actors.

When you write pronunciation down, you cannot use the ordinary alphabet, because there are not enough letters in it. English accents have over forty distinctive vowels and consonants, and as there are only twenty-six letters in the traditional alphabet, it is necessary to invent new symbols to cope with all of them. Over a century ago, scholars devised the International Phonetic Alphabet (IPA) to write down the sounds of any language in the world, and a version of this is available for anyone wanting to transcribe the sounds of any accent of English. It is the only system sufficiently sophisticated to handle all the nuances of sound that turn up. I have already used some symbols from it (p. 25). This is what I would have to use, I thought, if I were to write down EME exactly as it was.

I did spend a while thinking about a 're-spelled' version. This is a system in which only the letters of the familiar alphabet are used to sound out unfamiliar pronunciations. You see it a lot in dictionaries which want to avoid the use of phonetic symbols. For example, *station* might be written 'stayshun', *photograph* might be written 'fohtuhgrahf'. This would be impossible to use for EME, because some of the sounds then were quite unlike the sounds we have now, so modern spellings would not help. The EME vowel quality in *life*, for example – as we shall see in Chapter 3 – cannot be captured using Modern English letters. Re-spelling was out. It had to be a phonetic alphabet.

And that raised a huge pedagogical problem. I have often taught the IPA to students during university courses, and I know how long it takes. I would expect to make good progress after about ten weeks. It isn't something you can teach in a hurry. Students have to train both their ears and their mouths – to hear the differences between sounds and then to make them – and this needs practice, lots of it. I expected actors to be in the same position as university students. The only previous time I had done anything similar was when son Ben was training as an actor and we worked together on various dialect parts he had to do, which I wrote out in an IPA transcription. That hadn't been a problem – but Ben had previously done a degree in Linguistics and English Language at Lancaster University, so he was hardly typical! My impression was that most actors had done little phonetic transcription as part of their training. And with only four weeks in June to rehearse, a full IPA transcription of the whole of *Romeo and Juliet* didn't seem a realistic option.

It briefly crossed my mind that I might not do a written transcription at all. Perhaps all I needed to do was speak some Elizabethan texts (excluding *Romeo and Juliet*) in OP into a tape recorder, and get everyone to copy them – a sort of Linguaphone approach, which has a good track record when learning a foreign language. By repeated listening, the actors would pick up the sounds and gradually become fluent. They would then automatically transfer these skills to the *Romeo and Juliet* situation. No transcription needed.

But there was an unanswerable question: how long would it take for this process to work? I had no idea. I had never heard of a similar exercise being done before, so there was no one to ask. What I did know was that the claims of audio-method language-teaching publishers to 'teach you to speak a foreign language in three months' were pretty exaggerated, especially as far as pronunciation was concerned. And in any case, we didn't have three months. Probably less than one.

Perhaps I could adapt this auditory approach? Use it for just the one play, *Romeo and Juliet*. The actors would hear me read it aloud in OP and copy that. This thought occupied me for less than the time it takes to write it down. There were simply too many lines which could be read in more than one way.

Hundreds of places where my reading – the way I would emphasize certain words, for example – would inevitably select a particular interpretation of a line, at the expense of others. It would be possible to tell the actors, 'of course you can read it in any other way', but in practice they would find this difficult to do. First impressions count a lot. It might be quite a task to wean the actors away from the taped version.

There was, in any case, a more basic objection: the spectre of boredom was floating into view. The one thing I instinctively knew about OP was that it would be a truly exciting experience for anyone who encountered it. But this excitement would come only from the actors getting to grips with it and coming to 'own' it themselves. They would then add their own personalities, and their interpretation of their part, to make the text come alive. This is standard theatrical practice. But how on earth would they develop this sense of the 'life' of the accent if all they were able to hear was the same boring voice reading through the whole play, speech after speech, without special emotion or motivation? John Barton had told me how he had found Daniel Jones's reading of OP, despite its phonetic precision and consistency, flat and uninspiring. It would be the same with me. I might be able to have a go, given my age and temperament, at making the speeches of Old Capulet, or the Friar, come alive. But that was my limit. Juliet? I think not. There would be only one person who could make Juliet's speeches live in this way, and that would be the actress playing Juliet. I quickly concluded: it is the actors who have to breathe life into this accent, not the linguist. And that would require them to get to own the accent as soon as possible. This wouldn't happen from mere imitation. There had to be another way.

But the only other way was through a transcription. The actors would have to see their parts written down, and they would then interpret the text, just as they would when preparing their parts using conventional orthography. So what kind of transcription would work best? I had three versions of IPA in mind. The best thing, I felt, would be to present Tim Carroll with the various options, and let him choose. Then, once the choice had been made, the actors would work with a dialect coach who knew OP, just as they would with an unfamiliar modern dialect. It all seemed very straightforward, but I had a nagging doubt. And before I pressed 'Send' on my now unbelievably long email, I added:

All this presupposes someone who is able to listen and correct (or at least, consistentize) actor performances – a kind of Elizabethan dialect coach! Is this one for your Master of Voice?

It seemed unlikely. If this had been the remit of the Master of Voice, it would have happened already. And I reflected: it would have made no sense to involve me, if there were such a person already at the Globe? And then I reflected again: I hadn't heard of any such dialect coach, anywhere. A coach who was a specialist in EME? Such a being, in linguistic circles, would have been prized indeed. She, or he, almost certainly did not exist. And indeed, I thought, why *should* such a being exist, if this was the first time a theatre had done an OP production in fifty years?

I had spent over two hours on the email. It was enough. I suggested a meeting, and pressed 'Send'.

Meeting

We met three weeks later, at 2.30 on Friday afternoon, 6 February, in the Globe cafe. It is a splendid spot for a meeting. The cafe overlooks the river, and if you are short of ideas, you can always look at it flowing by or look across at St Paul's and suck in some inspiration. The view would also, I imagine, provide welcome relief if a conversation was flagging. No such risk on that afternoon.

There were three of us: Tim Carroll, Tom Cornford, and myself. Tom couldn't stay long, and Tim had to be away at 4, as he was still auditioning, so we had to cover a lot of ground quickly. The first thing I felt I needed to do was give them a sense of how EME sounded, so I read them the Prologue to *Romeo and Juliet*, in as natural an OP style as I could manage. There was a silence. Tim asked me to read it again. There was another silence. And then a stream of reaction, tinged, I felt, with not a little relief. People generally expect OP to be much more different from Modern English than in fact it is, and it comes as a bit of a surprise to realize that it is in many respects identical. It is certainly a noticeably different accent, compared with anything we have today, but the differences are no greater than between, say, Irish or Scots and RP. As we shall see in Chapter 3, almost all the consonants are the same, and several of the vowels. My audience of two had no difficulty understanding it. They were, understandably, relieved.

We talked through all the issues I had raised in my email, but the main thing was to decide on the issue of the transcription. I had brought with me a transcription of the Prologue using three methods. Here are the opening lines:

> Two households, both alike in dignity,
> In fair Verona, where we lay our scene,
> From ancient grudge break to new mutiny,
> Where civil blood makes civil hands unclean.

In the first version, every sound was transcribed into phonetic symbols, with the stressed syllables shown by a preceding '. It looked like this:

> 'tu: 'həʊshoːldz, 'boːθ ə'ləɪk ɪn 'dɪgnɪtəɪ,
> ɪn 'fɛːɹ və'roːnə, 'hwɛːɹ wɪ 'leː əʊɹ 'seːn,
> frəm 'ɛːnʃɪənt 'grɤʤ 'breːk tə 'njuː 'mjuːtnəɪ,
> hwɛːɹ 'sɪvɪl 'blɤd meːks 'sɪvɪl 'handz ən'kleːn.

I wasn't seriously suggesting this version for use, but I did think it was important that the directors saw a full transcription – if only to appreciate the benefits of the partial transcription which I showed them next. In this version, only those sounds which are in some way different in EME, or to which attention needs to be drawn, are given a phonetic transcription. It looked like this:

> Two 'haʊseho:lds, bo:th ə'ləɪke in dignitəɪ,
> In fɛ:ɹ Vero:na, hwɛ:ɹ wɪ le: əʊɹ sce:ne,
> Frəm ɛ:nʃɪənt grɤdge bre:k tə new mutnəɪ,
> hwɛ:ɹ civil blɤd mɛ:ks civil hands uncle:n.

It is immediately much easier to read. Of the 112 vowels and consonants in the first version, only thirty need a special transcription. Several words, such as *civil* and *two*, have not changed their pronunciation at all since Shakespeare's time, so they are left in standard spelling. Genuine differences in pronunciation can be seen in the strong *o* vowel in *Verona*, or the way the *i* is sounded in *ancient*, or the way the *wh* of *where* is pronounced with strong breath. The special symbols in such words as *we* and *from* are there for a different reason – to draw attention to the way they need to be said – rapidly and without emphasis – in the stream of speech. More on this in Chapter 3.

I also prepared a third version, which looked like this:

> Two <u>households</u>, <u>both</u> <u>alike</u> in dignity,
> In <u>fair</u> <u>Verona</u>, <u>where</u> we <u>lay</u> <u>our</u> <u>scene</u>,
> From <u>ancient</u> <u>grudge</u> <u>break</u> to new <u>mutiny</u>,
> <u>Where</u> civil <u>blood</u> <u>makes</u> civil hands <u>unclean</u>.

The underlining identifies a word which is pronounced differently in OP. An accompanying dictionary then gave the IPA transcription:

alike	əˈləɪk
ancient	ɛːnʃɪənt
blood	blʌd
both	boːθ etc.

There would be about 500 such words transcribed, I guessed, by the end of the play.

And I did one other thing. I showed Tim and Tom what a 'systemic' approach would look like, just in case they wanted to go down that road. This is an approach where, instead of learning the pronunciation word by word, and gradually building up a sense of what the distinctive sounds of the accent were, people learn the system of distinctive sounds at the outset. For instance, you point out that all words beginning with *wh-* had the *h* strongly pronounced – so that, for example, there would be a difference between *whales* and *Wales* – and then you leave it up to the actors to apply the rule to *why, when, whence, wherefore,* and all the other *wh-* words in the language. The same principle applies to vowels. You point out that the long *o* vowel in *Verona, both,* and *holds* is found in any other word which has the same vowel sound – *foes, overthrows, goes,* and so on. It is a rhyming approach, which can greatly speed up the learning of an accent. But it is an unfamiliar way of working, for most people, and it can take a while to get used to thinking of sets of words in this way. I didn't think actors would like it. They need to see words in context, from the outset, not isolated in a list.

It was a lot for Tim and Tom to take in. And no decision was made, that afternoon. But there was a lot of discussion about the dramaturgical implications. Should the noble characters sound different from the servants, in an age when accents were little affected by class distinction? Should the older characters sound different from the younger ones, in an age when pronunciation was changing rapidly? Should attention be paid to the unexpected puns which the transcription brought to light? 'I can tell her age unto an hour', says the Nurse about Juliet in Act 1, Scene 3. *Hour* was pronounced in exactly the same way as *whore* (that is why, in *As You Like It*, Jacques laughs for so long, after listening to Touchstone). Should something be made of this? There would be many such instances which would require a directorial steer. It was an exciting, sparky, multi-directional discussion. Possibilities piled on top of possibilities. We pencilled in various possible weekends in April and May for a seminar.

We overran our time, and Tim rushed off to his auditions. I don't know who was up for a part that day, but they may well have found the director somewhat distrait. For my part, I went for a drink ...

CHAPTER 3

Evidence

... with Globe Education. There was a small celebration taking place at 5 that afternoon in honour of Robert Dodsley, bookseller, writer, and Dr Johnson's publisher (amongst many other things), the 300th anniversary of whose birth had occurred with hardly anyone knowing about it. I must admit to not having noticed it myself. And it was the desire to rectify such ignorance that lay behind the invitation from Patrick Spottiswoode, the director of the Education department, to join him and a few friends for a glass or two of wine after I had finished my meeting with Tim Carroll. It was a delightful idea, for Dodsley was indeed a remarkable man – but that is another story – and we all learned a great deal, as we shared knowledge-fragments about him.

I left the theatre, several hours later, feeling that I could have played Juliet myself without any difficulty whatsoever, if only directors could see my potential. Globe Education parties are a bit like that. And I recalled three of the conversations I had had since 4 o'clock that afternoon.

Conversation 1 took place at 4.15 as I was passing the top of the stairs leading down to the Globe foyer. I bumped into one of the Practitioners – one of the team of professional actors who take part in Globe Education's outreach and on-site programmes for teachers, students, pupils, and others. 'What are you doing here?' he asked. I told him about the OP idea. There was a silence. Original pronunciation? 'But how do you know?' I gave him a potted version of the next few pages. As it was the first time I had been put on the spot like that, it was not entirely coherent, and it took ten minutes.

Conversation 2 took place at around 4.40 as I was meandering around the Globe bookshop, always a pleasant place to spend a spare quarter of an hour – and I mean, spend. I was in the process of paying for Peter Hall's new book when I realized I was standing next to someone who, out of context, I couldn't immediately place – but it turned out she had helped to steward my Sam Wanamaker talk a few months before. 'What are you doing here?' she asked. I told her about the OP idea. There was a silence. Original pronunciation? 'But how do you know?' I gave her a potted version of the next few pages. It was still not as systematic an answer as I would like, but at least it was a little more succinct. It took about eight minutes, this time.

Conversation 3 took place as soon as I arrived in Patrick's office, and was introduced to the first arrivals there. Patrick told them what I had been doing. There was a silence. Original pronunciation? 'But how do you know?' I gave them a potted version of the next few pages. It was a party, with a dozen conversations waiting to take off, so I speeded up my explanation. Gist, only. People seemed happy with gist, but I was not. I wanted to bend their ear for an hour.

'How do you know?' What is the evidence? That is what everyone asks, when you tell them about OP. And after the performances were all over, and I began my media round, it was the question which everyone asked first, on Radio 4, Radio 5, BBC News,

Richard and Judy ... So how *do* we know? You might think it is impossible to work out how people spoke 400 years ago. There were no tape recorders then. The earliest examples of recorded voices date from the 1870s. You can actually hear Florence Nightingale talking, on an early audio cylinder in the London Science Museum. But for anything before that, we need to be auditory detectives. There are three basic principles.

Spelling

The first principle is a general one, to do with what we know about how languages are written down and how they change over time. We have to assume that when people first write a language down they are trying to reflect the way it sounds. In the case of English, this happened in the Anglo-Saxon period, when Irish monks devised the alphabet. Scribes all over the country then used this alphabet to write their texts. And we can tell from the different ways in which they spelled a word that they pronounced these words differently. Spelling was immensely variable in those days.

We can then plot these spelling differences as the language changes, from Old English through Middle English into Early Modern English and thence into Modern English. We know how people speak today. So, we can also work backwards, deducing what earlier spelling variations must have meant. Spelling didn't really standardize until the eighteenth century, and before that it can be a helpful guide to how words were pronounced.

For example, in *Romeo and Juliet* how are we to say the final word in this line from Mercutio's description of Queen Mab (1.4.66)?

Her whip, of cricket's bone; the lash, of film

The Folio and most of the Quartos spells it *Philome*. It must have been a two-syllable word (as in Modern Irish). Or how should we take *poppering-pear* (2.1.38)? The First Folio spells it *Poprin Peare*. That tells us two things. *Poppering* must have had just two syllables. And there was no -g sounded in the -*ing* ending. More on this below.

Spelling is an especially important help when deciding how many syllables were in a word. The metrical structure of the line can help, too, but metre is of only limited assistance, because many lines have alternative metrical readings, and of course it doesn't help at all when we are dealing with prose. But when we see such spellings in the plays as *murdrous* for *murderous*, *desprat* for *desperate*, and *watry* for *watery* – and there are hundreds of them – it is plain that a reduced pronunciation was common. Often, the omitted letter is marked by an apostrophe – *murd'rous*, and so on – and this is a noticeable feature of printed editions which retain such forms as *t'have*, *i'th*, and *to't*.

Today, because of the influence of the standard written language, many people are uncomfortable when they hear sounds omitted that have letters present in the spelling. That is why, according to some, 'we should pronounce the *t* in *often*' and why the everyday pronunciation of *library* as *lib'ry* is often criticized as sloppy. This is Holofernes talking (in *Love's Labour's Lost*). The view that we should speak as we spell was just coming into English thought in the decades just before Shakespeare was born. Scholars and their disciples were beginning to follow this new rule, but most people didn't. And even when the spellings were written out in their 'full' form, there would have been no such pressure to sound out each one of them on the stage, as actors are routinely taught today. Many actors doubtless did so, and Polonius and Pistol are among those who probably would have approved of the 'mouthing' practice. But it wouldn't have been to Hamlet's taste. To have done so would have been the very opposite of speaking 'trippingly'.

Orthoepists

The second principle is the direct evidence we can obtain from contemporary accounts of the language. Sometimes Shakespeare's characters themselves comment, as when Holofernes talks about the various ways of pronouncing *calf* and *neighbour*. But more often the evidence comes from writers (known as *orthoepists*) who gave detailed accounts of pronunciation. For example, in John Hart's *Orthographie* (1569) we find a detailed description of the sounds of sixteenth-century English, and Ben Jonson included one in his *English Grammar*. How do we know that *r* was pronounced after vowels? Because Jonson is one of several who tell us so:

The dog's letter hirreth in the sound, the tongue striking the inner palate, with a trembling about the teeth. It is sounded firme in the beginning of the words, and more liquid in the middle, and ends; as in *rarer, riper*.

This tells us not only that *r* was pronounced after vowels, it also indicates that its pronunciation at the beginning of words was different from that at the end. In modern terms, we would say that initial *r* was a trilled sound, as often heard today in Scots and Welsh. The final *r* was, as Jonson said, 'liquid' (the term is still used in phonetics) – a continuant sound, much as is heard in West Country or American accents today. In my transcription, I used a special symbol, [ɹ], as a reminder that the letter needed to be sounded.

Why 'dog's letter'? This is a translation of a Latin expression, *littera canina*, for it seems the sound was pronounced that way in Latin too. Try imitating the 'grr' of a dog, and you will see how apt a description it is. There was actually an Elizabethan verb, to *arre*, meaning to snarl like a dog. And the usage was widely known, insofar as we can judge from the Nurse's comment (2.4.202):

NURSE: Doth not rosemary and Romeo begin both with a letter?

ROMEO: Ay, Nurse. What of that? Both with an 'R'.

NURSE: Ah, mocker! That's the dog's name. 'R' is for the –

Arse, as some have suggested?

Sound patterns

The third kind of evidence lies in the rhythms, rhymes, and puns used by the writers. We can deduce the stress pattern of a word from the metre of a line. We can deduce the value of a vowel from the way words rhyme. We can deduce whether a consonant was sounded from the way puns work. For instance, how should we pronounce the last syllable of *Rosaline* – to rhyme with *fin* or with *fine*? The text makes it clear (2.3.77):

ROMEO: Thou chidst me oft for loving Rosaline.

FRIAR: For doting, not for loving, pupil mine.

And other rhymes – with *brine* and *thine*, for example – support it.

Comparisons like this often have to be interpreted, of course. If we know that A rhymes with B, all we know is that the two words sounded the same: we do not know whether A sounded like B or B sounded like A. This problem comes to the fore when *both* the rhyming words are of uncertain value, as in this sequence (2.3.86):

> For this alliance may so happy prove
> To turn your household's rancour to pure love.

Did *prove* rhyme like *love* or did *love* rhyme with *prove*, or was the sound of both words something 'in between'? To decide this sort of thing, you have to look at the way these words were spelled, and how they rhyme elsewhere, and make a judgement. We find *love* rhyming with *dove* and *above*, in various parts of Shakespeare, but also with *move* (often spelled *moove*, suggesting a long vowel) and *remove*. Perhaps both pronunciations were current at the time. Or perhaps Shakespeare heard enough similarity between the words for them to count as a 'half-rhyme'. These were the kinds of cases I was thinking of when I said earlier (p. 20) that I was only 80 per cent confident about how EME sounded. I opted for full rhymes, in such cases, and made *prove* sound like *love*. Another historical linguist might conclude differently. This makes an important point: there is no one 'perfect' OP. Any OP version always incorporates dozens of personal judgements, alongside the decisions for which there is firm evidence, and several auditory alternatives are possible, as a result.

The next two lines in the play present a similar problem, but one which is easier to solve:

ROMEO: O, let us hence! I stand on sudden haste.
FRIAR: Wisely and slow. They stumble that run fast.

Was *fast* pronounced like *haste* or the other way round, or something in between? In the First Folio, *haste* is here spelled *hast*, the commonest spelling in those days. *Fast* rhymes with *last* in *Venus and Adonis* (lines 575–6), and with *past* in *The Rape of Lucrece* (lines 1668–71). There are a dozen or so places in the plays and poems where we can examine words which rhyme with *haste* and *fast*. The evidence plainly comes down in favour of both words sounding close to modern *fast*, as said with a short vowel [a], not the long 'ah' sound, [ɑː].

This kind of reasoning is routine in investigating OP. It is what leads us to conclude that the sound of *eyes* is heard at the end of *beauties*, that *feast* sounded like *best*, and that *one* sounded like *alone*. It requires meticulous detective-work, comparing all possible puns and rhymes. Fortunately, I did not have to do the basic work myself. That is the splendid achievement of Kökeritz, Dobson, and other historians of the language, over the past fifty years. I meant what I said when I talked about standing on shoulders.

You will thus appreciate my feelings of dissatisfaction during my brief Globe conversations. Linguistic topics by their nature are complex things. Many of the notions, such as 'half-rhyme' and 'metrical', are quite abstract. Even everyday words such as vowel and consonant pose problems, because people think of them as units of writing, not as units of speech. There are five vowels in English: *a*, *e*, *i*, *o*, and *u*. In written English, yes. But in spoken English there are twenty. People are not used to thinking in these terms (unless they have followed a course in linguistics). They need detailed illustration and careful explanation, and that takes time. A ten-minute conversation was nothing.

As I walked home along the South Bank that Friday evening, I did not realize how lucky I was. Four months later, I was standing in the wings waiting for my turn to appear on Channel 4's *Richard and Judy* show, to talk about the OP weekend. 'How do you know?' was one of the questions they wanted me to answer. 'How long do I have?', I had asked the show researcher. 'Oh, a good six minutes', she had said. What a beast I had been to chide at ten!

Decisions

It took the Globe a while to decide what to do. I wasn't surprised. It couldn't have been an easy time of year to be thinking of such things, with the new season just weeks away, casting to complete, and first rehearsals for the play starting at the beginning of March. With everything else needing to be decided – design and direction, cuts and costumes, movement and music – OP, and the luxury of a seminar, must have seemed somewhat secondary matters. Still, as time passed, I became increasingly anxious. I wanted to get on with the transcription, but without a steer from Tim, I didn't know which version to go for. I knew which edition of the play they were going to use (the New Penguin Shakespeare) but nothing about the cuts. There were bound to be cuts. No point in transcribing away if the lines were never going to be spoken.

An ominous e-message arrived from Tim a fortnight later. He was sorry for the delay. 'Too many loose ends ... and I can't tie many of them up just yet.' But the message contained a clue: 'We are having a meeting on Monday about OP, after which we should have a much clearer idea about how ambitious we can be. This in turn will affect what kind of transcription we ask for (what kind of simple transcription, that is), what date the seminar should be ... ' Ah, I seized on that, a 'simple transcription'. That had to be version 2. I thought of starting, then decided against it. They might still change their mind. And I still hadn't had any news of the cuts.

Next day, the cuts arrived from Tom Cornford. I was glad I'd waited. Around 700 lines had gone. Almost a quarter of the play. I had mixed feelings.

O heavy lightness! I hate all but the most essential of cuts. But deep inside, a little voice spoke: 'That's one week less transcribing that you'll have to do.' In such simple ways does pragmatics oversway principles.

But I still couldn't get on with the job without confirmation about the transcription. And in any case, Hilary (my wife) and I were off on a lecture tour the next day, which would take up the next week. When we got back, it was St David's Day. A new month, a new opportunity! I looked at the diary, and tried to work out how many evenings and weekends I had free before the beginning of May. I was down in London later that week – and such visits suck up more time than you might think, for Holyhead, where I live, is a five-hour train journey away. Then there was a trip planned to Stratford, to see Greg Doran's *Othello*. Then more lectures, in various places. And then it was the run-up to Easter, and I was on stage myself, in a performance of Neville Boundy's play, *Father and Son*, along with Ben, so there would be rehearsals of my own to fit in. I could see the next two months disappearing down an enormous plughole. I just had to start soon, or it would be too late. Time was passing. I listened. Time was passing. I so wanted to get on, but couldn't.

I emailed Tim. Had there been any developments? Only one: they had been unable to track down a dialect coach to work with the actors, and they were 'a bit worried'. They would be in touch soon. And they were. The good news: Tom Cornford communicated the decision about the transcription to me by email on 4 March. The bad news: the email never reached me. We were in the process of changing e-addresses in my office, and although everything should have been forwarded, this one didn't arrive. Don't you just love it, when that e-happens? I carried on with my travels, blissfully ignorant. There was a phone call from Debs Callan about the seminars: it now looked as if it wouldn't be possible to organize them in time. Instead, the plan was to have a 'talkback' session after each performance, at the end of June, and she hoped I would take part, along with some theatre specialists. A much better idea, I thought, especially if she could round up some of the people who had done such things before, such as John Barton and

Peter Hall. As we finished talking, I mentioned I hadn't heard anything about the transcription ye . . .

I was hardly able to blink before an email arrived from Tom, containing the missing news. 'We'd like a partial phonetic transcription using a combination of letters and phonetic symbols.' Splendid. He added: 'we thought this would be the simplest thing for a dialect coach to work from. In my experience, actors usually have their own notation for phonetics using letters. I guess that most of them will want to annotate their texts based on what they hear from the coach.' That was interesting, and it corresponded to what I had seen students do.

It was, I feel sure, the right decision – at least for this performance. A 'dual alphabet' transcription works well for actors who already know the lines by heart, and who have performed their parts in modern pronunciation several times already. It is not a question of their needing to read the lines from scratch, therefore, but of having an aide-memoire for those sounds which will be pronounced differently from what they are used to. The dual-alphabet system allows actors to skim over those words which are the same as today, and draws their attention to points of difference. I hoped it would work. The actors would, no doubt, tell me if it didn't (see Chapter 4).

The transcription took all my spare time from the end of March until the middle of May. In aggregate, I suppose about two weeks full-time equivalent. You might wonder why a mere 2,300 lines or thereabouts should take so long? Because it was by no means a mechanical task. Phonetic transcription is always a matter of making choices – was it this sound or that? should I use this symbol or that? – and EME was presenting all kinds of choices.

Styles

The most important choice, I felt, was the general style of pronunciation. How formal should the speech be? How fast should it be? All the evidence suggested that the general level of articulation in EME was much more casual and rapid than we would expect on a stage today. The abbreviated forms shown in texts (usually by apostrophes, as in *i'th'*) are a familiar indication of this – as well as such recommendations as 'speak the speech ... trippingly upon the tongue' and 'no mouthing'. The scholars seemed at one on this point. I therefore went for an informal style.

This style, I knew, would sound very different from what we are used to in traditional Shakespearian training and practice. There, 'little' words such as *of* and *my* are given prominence, consonants at the ends of words are clearly articulated, and consonants clustering together are kept sharply distinct. There should be no 'skidding across consonants', as Patsy Rodenburg puts it, in her excellent *Speaking Shakespeare* (p. 57). This is the modern way. But in Shakespeare's time, as many contemporary spellings show, they skidded.

Consonants would be dropped, especially at the ends of words: *frien(d)s, woulds(t) thou, clo(th)es, em(p)ty, gran(d)sire, as(k)ed, foun(d)st, mus(t)*, and so on. Vowels in the middle of words would be dropped, especially in the prose passages: *Greg'ry, meas'ring, unworthi'st, liv'ry, vari'ble, nat'ral*. Vowels would sometimes run together, as in *th' exchange*. It seems to have been an extremely colloquial style. And I therefore used these shortened forms throughout my transcription.

I also kept the 'little words' as short as possible – more technically, the 'grammatical words' which show the structure of a sentence, such as *of, to, by, the, for, been, from, I, he, him, her, she, my, mine,* and *them.* These are always weakly articulated in casual speech, unless there is a good reason to make them prominent. So I transcribed *and,* for example, as [ən] or just [n], suggesting a pronunciation which is still the norm in casual speech today, as seen in the common spelling *'n* (as in *fish 'n chips*). Spellings with *an* or *an'* are found in the plays. The phonetic symbol used here, [ə], represents the vowel sound heard in the usual pronunciation of the word *the,* or at the end of the word *sofa.* Known as 'schwa', in phonetic circles, it is the commonest sound in English, frequently heard whenever syllables are unstressed. I needed to use it often – for instance, to transcribe *of* as [əv] or – with the *f* missing – [ə]. You can hear this reduced form in present-day *cuppa tea = cup of tea.* It would have been widespread in EME too.

Pronouns, such as *I, me, my, mine, thou, his,* and *ye,* were especially affected by this tendency to reduce sounds in casual speech. Again, the spellings show it: *he* as *a*, *them* as *'em*, *his* as *'s*, and so on. In this style, such words as *my* and *thy* would have been pronounced [mɪ] and [thɪ] – an effect which is sometimes seen in modern English writing when we see such spellings as *me mother* or *thi dad*. Today, of course, such forms are considered non-standard, and are often criticized. They would not have been noticed in EME – some 200 years before standard English, as we know it today, was finally formed.

But this still leaves modern audiences with a challenge. When Romeo says, 'It is my lady. O, it is my love!' (2.2.10), it sounds like 'me lady' and 'me love', and we must be careful not to read in any association of uneducated speech at this point. Such cultural associations were nineteenth-century developments. Given Romeo's upper-class background, it might help to think of the words as *milady* and *milove*, with the 'uneducated' colloquial spellings replaced by 'educated' ones. But all such associations, educated or otherwise, are irrelevant, when it comes to listening to OP. They simply did not exist, for these sounds, in Elizabethan times.

The 'little words' make up a high percentage of all the words in a speech, and if they are being said rapidly, everything will move at a much increased rate. For Tom Cornford, this was one of the most 'challenging and thrilling' effects: reducing word-stress, he felt, 'had an intensifying, sharpening, and tightening effect on the show'. And for Tim Carroll, this was one of the main aims of the project:

I've spent a lot of my time as a director of Shakespeare trying to create a style of speaking in which the demands of the verse are really taken seriously – a style in which the actor is truly reluctant to stress a syllable in an unstressed position, and will only do so if the line cannot be understood otherwise. In the course of this quest, one of my bugbears has been the modern actor's insistence on stressing personal pronouns at every opportunity, when Shakespeare far more often wants to direct our attention to the verb or the noun. So for me it was bliss to hear Juliet say 'As sweet repose and rest / Come to thi *heart* as that within mi *breast*.'

The actors certainly felt the difference. For Kananu Kirimi (Juliet), the pace made her feel 'more muscular and immediate'. For Rhys Meredith (Benvolio), 'I felt like I was going for my actions a lot more strongly.'

And unexpected things started to happen. This is Jimmy Garnon's comment on the point:

The show went much quicker. Timings within scenes went awry because the OP moves quicker. All the Mi's and Bi's for My and By and all the shorter vowels and elisions shaved moments off speeches, so dances timed to last as long as other characters' exchanges were suddenly too long – in the case of the Capulets' party, far too long. The whole thing was more exciting somehow. Words felt like fireworks again. Little ones, it's true, but fireworks none the less.

The end result was that the OP performances, coming in at around two and a quarter hours, were about ten minutes shorter than those using modern pronunciation.

Challenges

Interference from modern ways of thinking about language presents repeated challenges to the ear, when we encounter OP. One of the greatest comes from the way speakers dropped their *h*'s. People have dropped their *h*'s at least since the Middle Ages, and it seems not to have bothered anyone very much until the eighteenth century, when the practice came to be considered uneducated – something done by Cockneys and other 'lower-class' people. Since then *h*-dropping has been avoided in careful educated speech. It isn't clear just how much *h*-dropping there was in EME, but spellings such as *Ercles* (for *Hercules*) and *ircanian* (for *Hyrcanian*) show that it was happening, as well as many such forms as *t'have*, *th'harmony*, and *an happy*. Spellings such as *a* for *he*, *all's* (= 'all his'), and *h'as* (= 'he has') show the same thing affecting the grammatical words. And Shakespearian rhymes such as *dinner* and *win her* or *art* and *heart* suggest it too.

I therefore left the *h* out of *he*, *him*, and *her*, unless there were grounds for special emphasis. That would hardly be noticed: it is no different from what happens today. Nobody pronounces the *h* in such unstressed contexts as *I saw her in town*. But should the *h* be dropped in such words as *happy* and *hence*?

It was beginning to be an issue, in Shakespeare's day. Sixteenth-century writers were already talking about the relationship between spellings and sounds. Shakespeare certainly knew about it. Holofernes (in *Love's Labour's Lost*, 5.1) is disgusted that anyone should pronounce *abhominable* without the *h*. And this shows that the matter was current. Holofernes wouldn't have been worried about it if the *h* was not being widely dropped as a matter of course. The orthoepists – and Holofernes may well have been modelled on one – were desperately anxious that people should pronounce all the letters in a word. They were laying the foundations for what would later be called 'correct' pronunciation. Some members of Elizabethan society would have tried to follow their recommendations (just as some people try to follow Henry Fowler's guide to English usage today); others would have ignored them. And this raises an interesting point of characterization.

The more well-educated members of English society would very likely have read some of the orthoepists' writings. Many would have been taught by them, or by their disciples. They would remember the recommendations of scholars such as Thomas Elyot, in *The Boke named The Governour* (1531, Chapter 5), who made it quite clear what should be done to a nobleman's son before he is seven. The nurses and other women about him, Elyot says, should 'speak none English but that which is clean, polite, perfectly and articulately pronounced, omitting no letter or syllable'. This applied even to those silent letters which had been added to a word to show their etymology, as in *debt* and *island*. Shakespeare was one of the first to poke fun at this, when he displays Holofernes' shock at the way the foreign courtier Don Armado pronounces his words. Here is the quotation in full:

I abhor such fanatical phantasims [extravagantly behaved persons], such insociable and point-device [affectedly precise] companions, such rackers of orthography as to speak 'dout', sine [without] 'b', when he should say 'doubt'; 'det' when he should pronounce 'debt' – 'd, e, b, t', not 'd, e, t'. He clepeth [calls] a calf 'cauf', half 'hauf', neighbour vocatur [is called] 'nebour' – 'neigh' abbreviated 'ne'. This is abhominable – which he would call 'abominable'.

It was an attitude by no means restricted to foreign visitors to court.

How might we apply such a climate of opinion to the characters in *Romeo and Juliet*? In Verona–England, we might imagine that the older, well-educated, and more conservative members of society – the Friars, the senior Capulets and Montagues, and especially the aristocratic women – would have been influenced by orthoepist opinions. Why women? Because we know from sociolinguistic studies that women are usually at the forefront of pronunciation change. If anyone was going to pronounce their *h*'s, it would be them. And, if Elyot's recommendations were being followed, so would their children.

I decided to try to reflect this possibility in the transcription. I kept the *h*'s in words used by the upper-class characters, old and young, and left them out in words used by the servants and other lower-class characters, such as the apothecary. This, I felt, would help convey the social divide to modern ears. And the Nurse? I made her drop her *h*'s too, but I later pointed out to Tim Carroll that this would depend on how she is played. If she were to be portrayed as an upper-class Victorian nanny, then perhaps they should go back in. In the end, they weren't needed in Bette Bourne's splendidly down-to-earth characterization.

A similar point of direction applied to emotional speech. When we are angry or excited today, our pronunciation becomes less precise. We omit sounds and run sounds together. Human nature has not changed that much in the past 400 years; it would have been the same in EME. So, when Capulet becomes furious with Juliet (in 3.5.167) and says, 'we have a curse in having her. Out on her, hilding!', might he have dropped his *h*'s in his rage? It is possible, but I felt that such decisions were for actors and directors, not linguists. I left the *h*'s in, in the transcription, and simply mentioned their omission as a possibility. In the event, Bill Stewart, playing Capulet, kept them in.

The use of *h* is not the only sound which presents a challenge to a modern audience. The loss of *-g* in the *-ing* ending of verbs is another general feature of EME colloquial speech, as in *ambling* [amblin] and *dancing* [dancin]. It had been like this since the Middle Ages, and you can see it in such First Folio spellings as *Poprin Peare* – for *poppering*. Elsewhere, Shakespeare puns on *reason* and *raising*, *mountain* and *mounting*, and many more. In the eighteenth century, the concern to pronounce the *g* became a major feature of educated speech, and its omission soon came to be associated with a lower-class usage perceived as 'lazy', as in *I ain't goin'*. (Curiously, it was also retained as an upper-class affectation, as in *huntin', shootin' an' fishin'*.) But none of these associations was present in EME, where *g*-dropping in the verb-ending was a widespread feature of colloquial speech. I used it throughout my transcription, for all characters.

Differences

I had to consider each EME sound separately – not just to get its phonetic value right, but to see what it might tell us about the characters and their relationships. It is an axiom of any phonetic study that people do not all speak in the same way. Men speak differently from women. Old people speak differently from young people. People from diverse social backgrounds speak differently. The differences affect not just sounds, but grammar and vocabulary too. 'The chief use of slang', it has been said, 'is to show that you are one of the gang.' Different gangs use different language. The members of a particular gang begin to speak like each other (the technical term is 'accommodate' to each other), and to make their speech different from other gangs. This has been studied by sociolinguists in a hundred different situations, from New York to

Turkey. The Capulets and the Montagues would have been the same.

So, a problem for any transcriber with a dramatic production in mind is how far to make the different social groups in *Romeo and Juliet* sound different. As people living in a particular period of English (aka Veronese) linguistic history, they would have shared the same 'core' of sounds. But they would not have been identical. Their age, in particular, would have been an important variable. The end of the sixteenth century was a period, all the evidence suggests, in which pronunciation was changing very rapidly. Within a generation, significant changes in pronunciation could be heard. Should these be represented?

To get a sense of rapid pronunciation change, we need only think of what is happening today. Differences between generations can be readily heard. My generation all said *schedule* beginning with *shed-*. My children, because of American influence, all say it beginning with *sked-*. There are dozens of these variations in present-day English. And there would have been many such variations in the 1590s. Old Capulets and Montagues would have spoken differently from the youngsters – somewhat more conservatively, as older people do today. We can imagine them telling off their children for using the latest 'cool' pronunciations. 'I don't want to hear you talking like that Tybalt', Capulet probably said, in an unsurviving Quarto.

Which sounds were changing in this way, around the year 1600? There was a great deal of variation in the way people said the vowel in such words as *not* and *God*. Spelling variations such as *doff* and *daff* suggest it, as well as such puns as *trap* and *tropically* in the *Hamlet* play scene (spelled *trapically* in the Quarto text). Some people evidently pronounced the vowel as it is today in British RP; others used a variant with the mouth more open, more like modern [a] – a pronunciation still heard in many American accents, 'Oh my Gaad!'. The [a] quality was the older form – the *a* spelling is normal in Chaucer – so it was probably more widely used among the older generation in Shakespeare's day. The younger generation would have been more likely to adopt the newer form. I therefore made this contrast systematic in my transcription, for example giving [Gad] to Capulet and [God] to Juliet.

The modern pronunciation of such words as *see, teen, sea,* and *peace* was also beginning to come in. Many younger people would have been saying these words as we do today, with an 'ee' vowel – symbolized as [i:] in IPA. Many older people would still have been using more open vowel qualities – more like the first vowel qualities you can hear in modern *say* [e:] or *Sarah* [ɛ:]. Because this vowel quality is very frequently used in English, the distinction between older and younger pronunciations could have been quite noticeable.

These distinctions have more than just phonetic interest. They can help to make a dramatic point, if the director wants. For example, I had the Nurse use the more conservative quality: her *Eve* and *teen* were written [e:ve] and [te:n], with the vowels sounding more like the one in modern *save* or *day*. Mercutio, on the other hand, uses the modern [i:] sounds. So, when he mocks the Nurse (2.4.104), he has a choice of mocking her accent too.

NURSE: My fan, Peter.

MERCUTIO: Good Peter, to hide her face

She says [peːteɹ] – 'pay-ter'. Mercutio would normally say *Peter*, as today, 'pee-ter' [piːteɹ]. The
option is therefore available for him to say [peːteɹ],
as part of his mockery – and to repeat the effect with
good-e'en a line or so later. It is a director/actor
decision – and one which, for this production, was
taken up.

As a third example of how things were changing
around the year 1600, we can look at such words as
musician, meditation, and so on. Today, the *ci* and *ti*
are pronounced 'sh' [ʃ]. In the sixteenth century, the
older pronunciation was 'see' – thus, 'mu-si-see-an',
'me-di-tay-see-on'. The [ʃ] pronunciation was steadily increasing its presence in English during this time,
as the spellings illustrate: in Shakespeare texts, for
example, we will find *lushious* for *luscious* and *mar-
shall* for *martial*. There was certainly a great deal of
variation in EME – just as there still is today, in such
words as *issue* – do you say 'iss-you' or 'ishoo'? But
though the new sound was coming in, the old sound

was slow to leave. Even as late as the 1620s, some orthoepists were recommending the pronunciation of these words in the old way.

It is therefore open to an EME transcriber to suggest a difference between conservative and innovative usage, in Shakespeare's time. We could assign the 'see' sounds to older speakers, and the 'sh' sounds to younger ones, thus contrasting 'mu-zi-see-ans' and 'mu-zi-shee-ans'. As I was anxious to draw attention to the diversity in the speech of the time, this is what I did. But I was being too clever. When Tim Carroll heard my final transcription, at the first rehearsal, he fell in love with the older pronunciation, and told everyone to use it. 'Master of Play' means what it says!

Features

Certain features of pronunciation would, of course, have been used by everyone in EME. Without a 'common core' of shared pronunciations, people would not have been able to understand each other. It is the same today. Despite all the variations between accents in Modern English, there is a great deal in common. Everyone uses a basic 'sound system' which in most respects is identical.

This is not to suggest that everyone spoke EME in a totally consistent manner. Again, there is an analogy with the present day. As already mentioned, I normally say *schedule* with *shed-*; but when I am talking to my children, who say *sked*, I accommodate to them, and say *sked-* too. Then, when they are not around, I find myself using both versions. In fact, I no longer know which I say more often. And similar alternative pronunciations can be heard in everyone's speech – *controversy* or *controversy*, *research* or *research*, *issue* or *ishoo*. EME would have been no different, with speakers unconsciously using competing pronunciations. These alternatives, of course, would have been a boon to poets interested in rhymes and puns, for it would allow them to associate different pairs of words as occasion demanded

There is clear evidence of the way many words had two pronunciations from the way they varied according to their position in a poetic line. In a regular metrical line, with five units of a 'te-tum' (iambic) character, a word can gain or lose a syllable depending on the rhythm. So, for example, in 1.5.102, *prayer* has to be a single-beat word:

Ay, pilgrim, lips that they must use in prayer,

But three lines later, it has to be a two-beat word:

Saints do not move, though grant for prayers' sake.

Similarly, *Mantua* is sometimes two beats ('mant-wa') and sometimes three ('mant-you-a'); *marriage* is sometimes two ('ma-ridg') and sometimes three ('ma-ree-ahge'). And above all, for this play, it is important to note that the names *Romeo* and *Juliet* can be either. The juxtaposition is very clear in 3.2.40–2, where *Romeo* in the first line has two beats, in the second line has two beats followed by three, and in the third line has three – to my mind, demonstrating an increasingly emotional tone.

JULIET: Can heaven be so envious?
NURSE: Romeo can,

Though heaven cannot. O Romeo, Romeo!
Who ever would have thought it? Romeo!

Note also that, in this analysis, *heaven* also varies: it has two beats in the first line and just one in the second.

Consonants

I turn now to the individual sounds, dealing with the 'easy' cases first. By 'easy', I mean those sounds which were the same then as they are now. They include almost all the consonants, and some of the vowels. The chief consonant differences I have already mentioned – the pronunciation of *r* after vowels, the dropping of final *-g* and initial *h-*, and the use of a strongly aspirated ('voiceless') *w* for words beginning with *wh-*. Another, very noticeable feature is the pronunciation of such words as *nature* and *torture*, which have no 'ch' [tʃ] in the middle: they are [neːtəɹ] – 'nay-tuhr', [toːɹtəɹ] – 'tawr-tuhr'. Similarly, there is no 'zh' [ʒ] sound in the middle of such words as *pleasure*: it is [plezəɹ] – 'ple-zuhr'.

This last example was something of a test case, for me. One of the best jokes in the play is when the Nurse, having been baited by Mercutio, says to Peter (2.4.151): 'And thou must stand by too, and suffer every knave to use me at his pleasure?' And Peter replies, 'I saw no man use you at his pleasure.' It gets a huge laugh in modern pronunciation. Would it, in OP, with *pleasure* pronounced so differently? I was delighted to see that it made not the slightest difference. At each performance, the audience roared.

There were a few other, more restricted differences. The *l* is absent in such words as *fault* and *shoulders*. There is a *t* [t] instead of a *th* [θ] in *loathsome*, *apothecary*, and *Balthasar*. The *v* could be dropped in *devil* [di:l]. There was no *y* in *lawyer* (the Quarto spells it *lawer*). The points are small ones, but cumulatively they add to the impression of an accent which is unlike anything we know today. The actors, as we shall see (p. 167), were certainly very sensitive to the importance of these individually different words.

Within each usage, there was of course scope for variation in EME. Judging by the comments of the orthoepists, the *-r* pronunciation was beginning to die out in London speech at that time. It would have disappeared completely by the time RP was formed, some 200 years later, leaving that accent as one of the few in the English-speaking world which do not pronounce -r after vowels. So, in Elizabethan England, there would have been several variations – some r's strongly pronounced, some weakly. And this allows directors the chance to introduce some linguistic character-notes. They have the choice of allowing the -r to be strong or weak. A strong pronunciation would remind modern listeners of rural, uneducated speech. A weak one would be much less likely to do so. And it would be legitimate to drop the -r altogether, if the requirement was to make a character sound modern.

In the *Romeo and Juliet* production, everyone pronounced their r's, but without particular emphasis. The reason, I suspect, as mentioned earlier, was the fear of overdoing it – of sounding too 'Mummerset' or 'Loamshire', as some of the cast described it. But everyone introduced them, and with great consistency – one of the most consistent features of the whole production, in fact. There was just one place where the r was omitted, and that was deliberate. It was when Mercutio, mocking Tybalt as a 'new tuner of accent', spoke the line 'By Jesu, a very good blade! a very tall man! a very good whore!' (2.4.30) in an affected modern RP. No -*r* for *whore*, in such an accent. The audience noticed, and the joke helped draw attention to the distance between EME and the present day.

Vowels

There are two main types of vowel in English: short and long. We can easily hear the length difference today in RP. Say *pit*, *pet*, *pat*, *pot*, *putt*, and *put*, or the unstressed vowel of *the*, and they take no time: the vowels are all short. Say *see*, *Sue*, *sir* (no -*r* in RP), *saw*, and the first vowel in *father*, and you can elong-ate them: the vowels are all long. Vowels which have two distinct auditory qualities (the *diphthongs*) are also all long: these are the sounds you hear in modern *say*, *lie*, *now*, *no*, and *joy*, as well as in *fear*, *tour*, and *fair* (again, with no -*r* in RP).

What were the equivalent vowel sounds in EME? Most of the short vowels were exactly the same. There was no difference in the vowels of *pit*, *pet*, and *put*, nor in the unstressed vowel of *the*. But the *a* of *pat*, *man*, *hand*, etc. was a little different – more like the present-day Northern British [a] than the RP quality, which (in the speech of the Queen, for example) is much further forward in the mouth, almost like the vowel in *set*. In phonetics, this modern RP sound is usually transcribed with an [æ] symbol, to draw attention to its *e*-like quality. It will often be heard in Shakespeare performances in modern (linguistic) dress. The pronunciation of *a* was much 'flatter' (technically, more open and further back) in EME.

The remaining short vowel, heard in such words as *putt, cup, love,* and *thus*, was rather different. In RP it is a somewhat open vowel, made towards the front of the mouth, and often transcribed with the symbol [ʌ]. In EME, the sound was much more central and further back (there are different opinions about just how far back it was). In my transcription, I used the rather strange-looking symbol [ɤ] to draw attention to this quality. It is difficult to describe in print: the quality is close to the sound of present-day Northern British *cup* [kʊp] but without the lip-rounding. Or, approaching it from another direction, it is a bit like [ə], but with a slightly darker or 'swallowed' quality, coming from further back in the mouth. I cannot be more precise than this, without an audio recording (for which, see the Internet source on p. 181). But the general point is clear: although such a quality can sometimes be heard today, notably in parts of the north of England, it is not widespread. It was, however, an important feature of EME speech.

Long vowels

The EME long vowels, like the short vowels, vary in the closeness of their relationship to Modern English. The [u:] in such words as *shoe, do, true,* etc. is the same as in a conservative RP accent today – that is, lacking the modern trend among young people to turn this sound into a diphthong and make it further forward in the mouth, so that *two* comes out almost like 'tyoo'. The [i:] in such words as *see* and *Peter* I have already talked about (p. 74): among older people, it was pronounced more like *say* and *pater*, but the modern pronunciation is perfectly acceptable as a norm for the period.

The vowel in such words as *father, car,* and *heart* is usually somewhat 'far back' in modern RP, and transcribed [ɑ:]. In EME it was pronounced further forward in the mouth, more like the [a] in *hat,* but longer, of course. Words like *laugh* and *staff* were pronounced in the same way – a long, open [a] quality. It is an important point to get right, as the [ɑ:] vowel is a very distinctive feature of modern RP, always exaggerated when comedians are mocking this accent. It is reflected accurately in the term 'far back' – for there is no open vowel pronounced further back than this.

The two remaining long vowels are more controversial. The first, usually transcribed [ɔ:], is heard in such words as *saw, law, all, brawls,* and so on. That was pronounced in a very similar way to today, but with the mouth a little more open (as happens often in Modern Irish). However, when followed by an *r*, as in *sort, form,* and *short,* it is unclear just what value was normal in EME. Two pronunciations seem to have been possible, the choice partly depending on the earlier history of the words: *form* with an [o:], as in modern *foe*; or *form* with an [ɑ:], as in modern *farm*. For the most part, I used the [o:] form in my transcription. But in a few cases, especially when following a *w*, as in *war* and *warm*, I went for the more open sound, without any lip-rounding – more 'wahrm' than 'wawrm'. An important word for *Romeo and Juliet* is *daughter*, and this too had an [ɑ:] – more 'dahter' than 'dawter'.

A similar uncertainty affects the vowel, usually transcribed [ɜ:], in such words as *bird*, *heard*, *person*, and *mercy*. This also had (at least) two pronunciations – one as today, and the other with an [ɑ:] – an effect that is sometimes conveyed in representations of colloquial speech – 'Marcy me!' It is an important one to get right, as so much meaning depends on it. The more difficult version, to modern ears, is the [ɑ:], for this would make *bird* sound like *bard*, *heard* like *hard*, and *person* like *parson*. In the interests of striking a balance (from the audience's point of view) between old and new, I retained the modern-sounding option in these cases.

Diphthongs

Another very distinctive feature of EME, compared with today, is the way the three common diphthongs were pronounced – those we hear in *tie*, *now*, and *toy*. In Modern English, they are often transcribed like this: [aɪ], [aʊ], and [ɔɪ], respectively. The [a] and [ɑ] symbols indicate that the mouth is very open for the beginning of the diphthong, in each case, and the [ɔ] symbol also represents quite an open quality. This is what was different, in EME. There, in each case, the diphthong began in the centre of the mouth, with the quality of the schwa vowel [ə]. So instead of [taɪ] we find [təɪ] ; instead of [naʊ] we find [nəʊ] – very close to the sound heard in modern Canadian English; and instead of [tɔɪ] we find, once again, [təɪ].

An alarm bell should be ringing at this point. Two different words with the same pronunciation? Yes, the sounds have come together. This often happens in language change over the years. The sounds we hear today in *see* and *sea* are the same, but a few hundred years ago they were different. Today, the sounds we hear in *tie* and *toy* are different; in EME they were the same. In linguistics, two words which are pronounced in the same way are called *homophones*. They are a major source of puns and word-play. Modern English has many examples: *deer/dear, hare/hair, son/sun, flower/flour* ... So did EME: *known/none, hart/ heart, gait/gate, dollar/dolour* ... It is so easy to miss the puns and word-play of an earlier linguistic age, because of pronunciation change. The *Romeo and Juliet* Prologue provides an early example of the *toy/tie* identity. 'From forth the fatal loins of these two foes ...' *Loins* here would have been pronounced in the same way as *lines* – and the play on words is obvious.

The [əɪ] sound was very noticeable in EME because it was also used at the ends of words where today we use an [i] vowel – such as *lively*, *ready*, *happy*, and *chastity* – and there are many of them. It would remind a modern listener of the sound in the word *eye*. But in most such cases the diphthong is in an unstressed syllable, and should be spoken very rapidly. Although this may well have been a bit old-fashioned in 1600, that quality has to be there, otherwise the rhymes don't work, as in Juliet's conclusion to Act 3:

> I'll to the Friar to know his remedy.
> If all else fail, myself have power to die.

The remaining diphthongs can be heard in the words *say*, *go*, *fear*, *tour*, and *where*. The two qualities in these sounds can be clearly heard in Modern English, especially if the words are said slowly – roughly 'say-ee' [eɪ], 'goh-oo' [əʊ], 'fee-uh' [ɪə], 'too-uh' [ʊə] , and 'whair-uh' [ɛə]. But in EME these auditory movements were missing. The sounds were 'pure' vowels – that is, pronounced with a single auditory quality throughout. *Say* was [se:], the kind of sound you hear in French *bébé*, but also in Yorkshire, for example. *Go* was [go:], very common in regional English today, such as in Wales and Scotland. The three other diphthongs, in *fear*, *tour*, and *where*, do not sound very different from their modern pronunciations because of the way the tongue moves to pronounce the following *r*, but they do have a longer, tenser sound – [fiːɹ], [tuːɹ], and [wɛːɹ], respectively. You hear something similar in Scots.

Individual cases

The preceding sections contain the general observations which need to be made about the consonants and vowels of EME. In addition, a number of words have to be thought about on an individual basis, just as in Modern English. Today, the word *garage* can be pronounced in two ways – roughly 'ga-rahge' and 'ga-ridge'. No other word in the language varies like this. It is a unique case. And in EME there were several such cases. What to do with *zounds*, for example? I looked at various possibilities, then chose [zwu:ns] – not least, because it is spelled *zwounes* in the Quarto version of the play (3.1.48).

These individual words do not turn up very often, but they do add a great deal, in aggregate, to the colour of EME. For example, *quoth* and *banquet* appear without the [w] – 'koth' and 'banket'. *Cousin* has the first vowel sounding like the *o* of *hot*. *Fellow*, *morrow*, and other such words have an ending with 'uh' [ə], not 'oh' [əʊ]; this is still heard today in the pronunciation represented by the (non-standard) spelling, *fella*. *None*, *one*, and *nothing* all had an 'oh' [o:] vowel – something that is needed for the rhyme at 2.6.36–7.

> For, by your leave, you shall not stay alone
> Till Holy Church incorporate two in one.

Resonances

When we add all these consonant, short vowel, long vowel, and diphthong qualities together, we obtain the sound system that I have been calling OP. It is an interesting accent, to modern ears, because people hear all kinds of different regional echoes in it. For example, the short [a] pronunciations add a distinctly Northern British resonance to the speech, reminding listeners of Lancashire or Yorkshire. But a similar [a] sound was also used in such words as *any* and *many*, and after [w] in such words as *what*, *want*, and *watch*, and this pronunciation is common in many Irish accents. That is why people hear different resonances in EME speech. Listen to some words, and they remind you of modern accent A; listen to other words, and they remind you of modern accent B.

In all, there are resonances of about a dozen modern accents in EME, thanks to the way the sound structure of individual words has pulled vowels in different directions over time. Such words as *yes*, *yet*, and *yesterday* had their *e* vowel pulled in the direction of [ɪ], making them sound like present-day Australian. *Neither* and *either* both had a short vowel, [nethe.ɪ] and [ɪthe.ɪ], which might remind you of some Scottish accents. And I have already mentioned (p. 73) the way many people pronounced the short vowel in *hot*, *not*, *long*, etc. with a more open mouth and without any lip-rounding, as most Americans do.

The actors were enthralled by these resonances. This was Kananu Kirimi's first impression:

I found OP a lot more encompassing than I'd imagined. I thought it would be one specific way of pronouncing things, and if you couldn't mimic that you'd be a bit off. So I loved the way it seemed to go from one place to another, from phrase to phrase – West Country, Irish, Scottish, Northern blending into one another. That excited me. There was choice, and it included the entire country.

And beyond. For Joel Trill (Escalus), whose family background is West Indies, 'I was very surprised at how close it sounded to Caribbean.' And he added: 'As someone playing a high-ranking character, the option of using an accent other than RP was immensely liberating.'

The audiences heard these resonances, too, and readily identified with them. In fact, one of the most noticeable features of the talkback sessions after the OP performances was the way people associated EME pronunciation with an accent they knew. Everyone felt at home with it, but for different reasons. The conclusion is obvious: *no* modern accent is identical with EME. All share some features, for the simple reason that we are talking about an accent (more precisely, a group of accents) which is the ancestor of the accents we hear in English today. And not just British English, but English all over the world. Captain John Smith and his settlers would arrive in Virginia in 1606, the year (we believe) that Shakespeare was writing *Macbeth*.

All accents have changed since then, of course. The American English heard in Virginia today, even in its most conservative forms, has moved a long way from that which arrived in 1606. After 400 years of language change, it could hardly be otherwise. And the same applies to British accents. No modern accent has miraculously preserved all of Shakespeare's pronunciation. To think otherwise is one of the biggest linguistic fallacies of modern times. And yet it is surprising how widespread is the belief that Real Elizabethan English is alive and well, tucked away

in a remote valley somewhere in Virginia – or
Warwickshire.

There is a grain of truth in the myth. Sounds do
not all change in the same way and at the same rate.
Some, as we have seen, have not changed at all. So it
is not surprising that modern accents have retained
some resemblances to EME. That is why it is important to talk of 'resonances', or 'echoes', when comparing EME to present-day English.

The transcription took a long time. After I transcribed each line, I read it aloud, several times, to
see if it 'worked'. It took me three drafts before I was
satisfied. And even then I kept wanting to tinker
with it. But the tinkering had to stop. May was only
a short time away. I had a moment of panic. What if
I had got everything completely wrong? I emailed an
old friend, John Wells, Professor of Phonetics at
University College London, and asked him if he
would read it through and point out any awful
blunders. He was just off to China, but only for
ten days, and he promised to look at it, along with
my accompanying notes (written for the benefit of

the directors and the still-hoped-for dialect coach), when he got back. He was as good as his word. He read it straight away, and I was greatly relieved that he had only a few small suggestions for change. I made the changes in the transcript, printed it out, and put it on one side for a week. I needed a break from it. As May turned, I read it once more. It had kept its freshness. I sent it in.

CHAPTER 4

Rehearsal

The transcription, and its accompanying commentary, went off to Sid Charlton, the general manager at the Globe, on 14 May. In fact, I sent two. The complete text ran to over eighty pages, and I figured that no actor would want to see all of it. So I sent one complete copy to Sid, for circulation to Tim Carroll and Tom Cornford, and reworked the transcript on a character-by-character basis for the actors, printing out all Romeo's lines in one text, all Juliet's in another, and so on. Some of the actors were doubling up roles, so I was also able to group their parts together. Elizabethan cue-scripts, evidently, worked on the same principle.

I thought the actors would appreciate this approach (as indeed they did). Romeo would be able to concentrate on his part without being bothered by anyone else's. And the same with the others.

Apart from convenience, I thought it might actually cut down on the risk of interference. Recall that the transcriptions were not all the same (p. 72). If Romeo, getting to grips with his transcription, saw that the Friar had a transcription which differed from his, it might have been confusing. But, apart from that, these part-transcripts had an unexpected benefit for me. Seeing all the lines of a particular character together enabled me to spot a few inconsistencies I hadn't noticed before.

There had been no opportunity to discuss any of this with Tim or Tom beforehand. The opening night of *Romeo and Juliet* had been 7 May. Try reaching a theatre director a few days before opening night to talk about some special performances over a month off? Not a chance. I was, I thought, on my own.

Then, some good news. They had found a dialect coach – Charmian Hoare, well known as a teacher on the English drama-school circuit, and a hugely experienced dialect coach, having worked often for the RSC and many other companies. We talked on the phone, and I sent her a copy of the transcript. OP was completely new to her, but it was obvious, after only a few minutes' chat, that here was somebody who would have no trouble assimilating a transcription and translating it into workshop practice. She did mention one point, though. A tape would help, she thought.

I had rejected the idea of a tape recording very early on in the year (p. 31), but this was different. This wasn't to be a tape which the actors would totally rely upon. It would be a tape which would act as an aide-memoire for Charmian, and also one which the actors could refer to on occasion, when they were on their own – but only *after* they had worked with her on their performance. It seemed like a good idea, and so I asked Tom Cornford to set it up. The first rehearsal for the OP performances had been scheduled for the afternoon of Thursday 27 May. I could be down in London and do the recording during the morning of that day, if that was convenient? It was.

From the actors' point of view, the 27th was a good choice of day. The Globe's production of *Much Ado* had gone up on the 23rd, and was performing nightly that week, so the R&J company had four days off. Time to accumulate some mental energy, I hoped – because they would need it. The first OP performance was on Friday 25th. That was twenty-eight days away. During that time they were doing the play fourteen times – including a midnight performance for Midsummer's Day. Somehow they would have to find the time and energy to relearn their parts, at a technical phonetic level, then rethink their parts – for, I surmised, the new sounds and rhythms would surely influence their behaviour on stage. I had no clear idea what effect it would have on their interpretation of the lines, or of their characters, but everything I had learned about acting told me that there were bound to be some consequences. I did not realize just how far-reaching these consequences would be (Chapter 5).

Mark Rylance had thought that four weeks would be enough rehearsal time for an OP production. It turned out he was right – but it was a tight four weeks, and it would have benefited from a little more. As it was, Charmian was able to devote only two to three hours working with each actor. It is a real testimonial to the professionalism of this cast that they managed it so well. The talkback audiences were

amazed when they were told that the whole OP production had come together in less than a month.

And this makes a good point to record the names of
the cast, as they appeared in the Globe programme:

Prince Escalus	Joel Trill
County Paris, Gregory	Callum Coates
Mercutio	James Garnon
Capulet	Bill Stewart
Lady Capulet	Melanie Jessop
Juliet	Kananu Kirimi
Tybalt	Simon Müller
Nurse	Bette Bourne
Peter	John Paul Connolly
Montague, Apothecary	Terry McGinity
Lady Montague	Julia Marsen
Romeo	Tom Burke
Benvolio, Friar John	Rhys Meredith
Balthasar	Tas Emiabata
Friar Laurence	John McEnery

I had met none of them before. Nor had I had a chance to get down to London to see the production before the OP weekend. The rehearsal on the 27th would be a first encounter, for all of us.

I didn't know whether the actors were looking forward to it or not. In fact I now know that, on the whole, they were not. Bette Bourne told me frankly afterwards: 'Quite a few of us went around bitching the whole idea at first ... "Well, *I'm* just going to do *this*, and if they don't like it they can **** themselves." Another said "I'm just going to do it drunk!" Yes, we were very sweet about the whole thing ... ' And for himself, he commented: 'having spent many years thinking about the nurse, and working on her for three months, to change all that in two and a half weeks seemed to me to be insane – and coming from an academic naiveté about how actors work'. John Barton recalled a similar theatrical suspicion of his own academic connections when he was at Cambridge.

If there was a shared attitude, it was not so much antagonism as puzzlement. This was Rhys Meredith's (Benvolio) feeling:

When I heard about it, I was at first a little confused, as it seemed to be quite a strange thing for Tim to want us to do, as he is so keen for us to speak truthfully in our 'own voice', and to be honest, knowing nothing about OP it conjured up dated notions of Mummerset accents superimposed on the text in order to make up for an inability to make the text amusing in and of itself – a kind of 'funny voice acting'. People were saying things like 'I heard it was just like Devon' or 'It's a mix of American and Irish' – the kind of half explanation and wild speculation that actors like to engage in. The more that filtered through to us, the more concerned I got. It's all very well doing a single accent, something we have heard and have a reference for, but to attempt something that was beginning to sound like an amalgam of all the accents under the sun was a little worrying. I was holding on to the fact that if it was the worst case scenario and it turned out to be absurd, at least we would have only to do it the three times. This perhaps overemphasises my trepidation. I was intrigued, too, as I didn't suppose that Tim would embark on anything without good reason; so 'intrigued with reservations' probably best describes my feelings.

And probably the feelings of several others too. There would have been a real anxiety over whether they could do it in time, whether they were up to it, and a host of other considerations. All actors worry – usually unnecessarily – but they worry nonetheless. So I was not surprised to learn, afterwards, that several of the cast, on arriving in the rehearsal room that day, were experiencing varying symptoms of panic.

I knew none of this, I'm relieved to say. If I had, I might never have gone through with it! Nobody likes to walk into a class of antagonistic professionals. But, anticipating that there might be some problems, I had a cunning plan. I would not show them the transcription until I had completed a softening-up process. I would give them an entertaining mini-lecture on linguistic life and times in Elizabethan England ... read a few extracts to them ... make them feel at home in it ... and only then show them the script. Then we would work our way through the sounds, gently, one at a time ... in much the same way as I have described them in Chapter 3 ... then they could have a go themselves. The crucial thing, I said to Sid, when I arrived at the Globe on the Thursday morning, was that they MUSTN'T SEE THE TRANSCRIPTION FIRST. I could imagine a universal exodus, if they did.

There was one other thing to do, before I could record. A couple of days earlier, Tom Cornford had emailed me to say that there had been a few more cuts, and some additional lines had been added. Nothing major, but it meant a bit of last-minute transcribing. No time for research now. I had to do it on the fly. Fortunately, none of the new words posed any problems.

In fact, even after the recording, there proved to be a bit more transcription to do. The Globe has a practice, like many theatres, of asking people at the beginning of a performance not to photograph the performance, to switch off mobile phones, and so on. One of the actors always does this. Just before the show went up I got a call from stage manager Bryan Patterson: they'd like to do the announcement in OP. Fine. There was no mention of 'mobile phones' in Kökeritz, but I reckoned I could manage it. I sent it in.

Then they changed their minds – I don't know why – but the change allowed John Paul Connolly, who made the announcement, to carry off a nice joke. He's from Armagh, and his native accent is Northern Irish. He came on, welcomed the audience to the performance 'which will be in original pronunciation', and then added: 'in case you're wondering, we haven't started yet; I always talk like this!' It got a good laugh each time – and actually, I think, in its small way, helped to demystify the occasion.

And I must record, at this point, the way the company started the play, for it was one of the most effective openings I have ever seen. John Paul was dressed as one of the Capulets. He finishes his announcement, and is about to leave through the door upstage right, with a fellow Capulet, when downstage left arrives Tas Emiabata, dressed as one of the Montagues, with a fellow Montague. Tas starts to make the same announcement that John Paul has just made. JP hears this, and remonstrates with him. 'It's the Montagues' turn to make the announcement today', says Tas. 'No it isn't', says John Paul. The audience roars. The two Capulets and Montagues begin to argue loudly about whose turn it is, then the Capulets turn away in disgust. As they cross the stage, John Paul looks back and bites his thumb at the Montagues in disgust. 'Do you bite your thumb at me, sir?' We're off.

That's right. There was no prologue. And the first forty-two lines of the Sampson/Gregory dialogue were cut. Some will lament. But it made for a fine pacy start, and introduced a dynamic which I felt held up throughout the play.

Meeting

On the 27th I spent the morning in the management offices, upstairs at the back of the theatre, in the room variously called, because of its large glass window, the 'jam jar' or the 'anchovy bowl' (because – what's in a name? – it is a mini-version of the adjacent, even more windowful 'goldfish bowl'). Tom Cornford had set up two tape recorders, and there was a copious supply of tapes. I did a few lines in front of Tom, to see if they were at the right pace and level. He thought they were, and left me to it. I started just after 10 and finished about 12.30. Two hours, traffic indeed. But that's two and a half, do I hear you say? Ah, but there were fluffs, you see. Quite a few, in fact. Well, I had never recorded a whole Shakespeare play at one go before, not in any P, let alone OP. I wondered whether to cut them out and

re-record, but decided against it. Apart from anything else, it would show the actors that even linguists are human. It did seem to have a reassuring
effect. Kananu Kirimi told me afterwards that the
fluffs were some of the best bits.

In case anyone tries to use this procedure again, I
should issue a word of warning. Listening to tape
recordings can do strange things to your state of
mind. Tom Burke (Romeo) said that one night,
during the rehearsal period, he put his tape recorder
on as he fell asleep. This is a recognized technique,
actually, used in some methods of foreign language
teaching: 'learn while sleeping', goes the slogan. The
only thing was, it gave him nightmares! Queen Mab
on the rampage again. He saw himself on stage,
surrounded by the cast, all haranguing him in OP.
And every one of them had my face!

I talk of dreams ... By contrast, lunch with
Charmian that day was a very realistic affair. This
was our first meeting, and we had to get to know each
other and work out a way of proceeding. She knew
how to work with actors much more than I did. On
the other hand, this was the first time she had worked

with OP. I explained the method I was proposing to use, and she concurred. We both wanted it to be a very informal occasion, with everyone chipping in as the spirit moved them. We thought they would. Ever encountered an unforthcoming actor?

The rehearsal was being held at 2, in one of the rooms in 135 Park Street, a short distance from the theatre – across New Globe Walk and round the corner. It was to be a four-hour session. When we arrived, the actors were there already – all bar one, who was unwell – and so were Tim Carroll, the stage manager Bryan Patterson, and members of his team. It was a long thin room, which had been laid out academic style, with a lecturing space, flip-chart and pens in front of a few rows of chairs. I came in through a door at one end of the room, and saw a blur of people on the chairs. But one thing I saw clearly. One of the Globe team had the personalized transcripts. And she was giving them out. To the actors. One each. My message, evidently, hadn't got through.

By the time I reached the middle of the room, I could see the faces. They weren't looking at me. They were staring at the transcripts. I don't think I have ever seen such a frozen set of faces! I thought quickly: on to Plan B. Then I remembered. There was no Plan B. So when Tim introduced me, all I could do was tell them not to worry, to put the transcripts away for a while, and just listen. I brought forward my reading of the Prologue and went through a fair chunk of the first scene of the play. There was noticeable relief. As I've said before, this always happens: people think OP is going to be harder than it is. As Rhys Meredith recalled: 'I was amazed that I understood every word, and followed it so easily, and indeed, how natural it sounded. It was a single accent. Despite all the sounds that you could hear from all the different regions, it held together.' And Jimmy Garnon's first impression 'was surprise at how readily I could understand it, and a delight in those words (such as *one* and *none*) that seemed more obscure'.

I spent the first twenty minutes or so talking generally about linguistic practice on the Elizabethan stage, insofar as we knew. I stressed the points about pace and colloquial effect, described above. There were several questions. The cast homed in straight away on some of the most salient points, especially the different social class resonances of OP and RP. There was a mixture of native accents in the room, and people noticed the points of similarity. There was a great deal of hilarity and mutual accent mocking. I was greatly relieved. The initial panic slowly died away.

Some of my points were particularly reassuring, I learned later. As Rhys Meredith recalled:

It helped to hear that London of the period was a melting pot and that the accent was prone to variation, and that it would be entirely natural that our own regional accents should not fall by the wayside but form a part of the OP as a kind of base on which some of the more unusually pronounced words should sit . . .

And one of my throwaway remarks turned out to be more useful than I knew:

. . . and furthermore that nobody would know if we were doing it wrong.

Well, that's a certain text.

I explained why we needed a transcription, and how I'd done it. Then I went through the distinctive sounds, one at a time, identifying the special symbol each one had, and giving lots of examples. Having been knocked off balance a bit by the absence of Plan B, I got into a muddle at one point, and began to explain two diphthongs together which really should have been kept apart. Charmian was onto it like a flash. It was immensely reassuring to me to have her there.

Tim Carroll was listening along with the others, and his role at this stage was crucial. I had left open several issues – as the outline in Chapter 3 will have illustrated – and they had to be discussed. How strongly were those *r*'s to be pronounced? Were people happy about the differences between older and younger speech, such as [iː] vs [eː] (p. 74)? How rapidly should everyone speak? What about the 'see' vs 'sh' distinction in such words as *musicians*? This was the first real chance to discuss these points in detail – the first chance for me to see whether each of my decisions would be dramaturgically real. Stylistic decisions are always hypotheses, and in the theatre the evidence which validates them lies in the minds and mouths of the director and actors, and – later – in the ears and hands of the audience.

Tim stressed the importance of maintaining pace and a natural rhythm. This included vocal inflection (intonation), about which we know nothing by way of OP (p. 13). He had no problem with the actors letting their natural tone of voice influence their accent. If a Scottish lilt were to appear in Juliet, from time to time, that was fine. He also resolved a few of my pronunciation options. For instance, after hearing the two options for *musician* (p. 76), he asked everyone to go for the older ('mu-zi-see-an') form. Given that there was a choice, and an uncertainty about how fast this change had been travelling through English in the 1590s, he felt the older form added greatly to the overall auditory character of the accent. 'Audiences will come to an OP performance expecting the accent to be different', he commented, 'so in cases where there is a choice, let's go for the more distinctive sound.' Fifty years before, this had been John Barton's reasoning too.

Not all of the issues could be resolved that afternoon. Actors have their individual ways of working, and many points relating to characterization would have to wait until the private sessions with Charmian. Bette Bourne (Nurse) told me afterwards how he was unable to do much that afternoon. He likes to spend a lot of time in private preparation for a part, so that when he presents it for the first time in rehearsal he has already done a great deal of the donkey-work. I think several actors work like this. So I wasn't sure that the procedure I intended to use in the second half of the afternoon would be success-ful. It worked well enough in university classes with aspiring phoneticians. But actors?

We had a tea break around 4 o'clock. Afterwards, my plan was to get each member of the company to come up front and read a few lines of their part in OP, cold. Charmian had a better idea. 'Let's do some unison speech first', she said. This wasn't a technique I'd used before, but it proved to be immensely help-ful. I wrote up the Prologue on the flip-chart in the transcription, read it over a couple of times, and then Charmian conducted a chorus. They did it twice, and I was amazed at how, already, I could hear the accent beginning to emerge.

And that is how the rest of the afternoon went. One by one the cast came up, and had a go. Some focused on one type of sound, some on another. The first few lines faltered, then they picked up speed and accuracy. There was no attempt at fluency or interpretation, of course. It was a mechanical exercise. I corrected gross errors on the spot, every time I heard one, and let minor discrepancies go by without comment. The long [oː] words caused most difficulty – [noːn] for *none*, [floːɹ] for *flower*, [oːn] for *one*, and so on – and they had special trouble with the new [əɪ] quality for 'oi' in such words as *boisterous* and *poison*. The [əɪ] of *like* was a nuisance: there was a tendency to round the vowel, and make it into an Irish 'loike'. They found it difficult to leave behind the 'ch' in such words as *torture*, *fortune*, and *opportunity*, and the 'zh' in the middle of *measure* and *leisure*. Several of the 'see-on's (*affection*, *salutation*) were missed, and they kept their *g*'s at the ends of *-ing* forms. On the other hand, everyone had picked up the *wh-* sound, and they seemed to adapt almost naturally to the extra pace and liveliness which arose from using the unstressed forms, such as [mi] for *my* and [n] for *and* (p. 62).

As the clock approached 6, there was little left to do. Charmian had to fix up times for individual sessions. People had to collect their tapes. There was a rehearsal call for the next day (for the usual production). I arranged to come back three weeks later to do follow-up work in the final rehearsals immediately before the performance weekend. Everyone was told they could go.

And gosh, did they go! I went to the gents, and when I came back everyone had disappeared, apart from some members of the management team, who were clearing up. I suspect the pub round the corner was full. I was hugely heartened by what I had heard. Most of the company were getting it largely right first time, and nobody was a disaster. With this kind of progress, in an afternoon, I felt maybe twenty-eight days wouldn't be too short after all.

Refining

But there was still an enormous amount to be done. It's one thing becoming familiar with an accent. It's another thing to own it. The difference is this. Any competent parrot can imitate. Learning a set of lines in a particular accent requires little more than a good ear, memory, and tongue. Ownership, by contrast, implies the ability to be creative – to be able to use the accent in relation to new language, and not be restricted to the language of the lines. The aim is to be able to speak the accent in any circumstances, not just those within the play. So, thinking ahead, when I was in the Green Room with Charmian before the first performance, both of us trouble-shooting last-minute queries, I was really delighted to hear one of the actors jocularly greet another in perfect OP, and to hear the corresponding reply. When people start to play with an accent or dialect, then they truly can be said to own it.

How did Charmian get on? She found the task much easier than she had expected. The tape turned out to be a boon. The hardest part, she said after-wards, was 'encouraging them to get the precise placement of the vowels – like the one in *why* and the *home* and *stay* vowels. They wanted to generalize into a sort of West Country sound, and my task was to encourage them to be more specific.' How she did it was recalled by Rhys Meredith later:

We were divided into groups with Charmian, and what immediately became apparent was that our regional variations were coming to the fore. For instance, Simon had a facility for the Northern sounds, Joel had a real capacity to bring out the Devon sounds, and Jimmy and I would send one another more and more towards Ireland (although neither of us are Irish – just susceptible to influence, I guess). This was happening so much that Charmian would use each of us as examples to the others on how to produce certain sounds, and so try to bring about more of a convergence. After a couple of sessions going away practising our weaker sounds and not overemphasizing our strengths, there was more of a uniformity without losing our 'own voice'.

The actors were all aware of the problem. Each found some sounds to be much harder than others, but not everyone had trouble with the same sounds. Charmian was surprised that 'the older actors found the *e* vowel in *even* and *please* rather tricky' (the use of [e:] instead of [i:], p. 74). And she added: 'I wish I'd had more time to have really gone for those sounds, especially as so often they encourage a rhyme which in modern speech is not there.' In fact, in the performances the actors got them right most of the time, but there was a degree of inconsistency, it has to be said.

A general point can be made. Problems of inconsistency arise not so much in the quiet reflective passages or everyday dialogues as in the moments of high emotion or great action. It is a familiar point to those who have studied language acquisition in young children. A two-year-old can produce a sound, word, or piece of grammar perfectly fine while sitting quietly, but lose it when walking around or carrying out some other activity. 'Walk then talk' or 'talk then walk' – but not both at once – is an aphorism often heard in relation to infants. It is the same with adults learning a foreign language – and, as here, learning a new accent. This is where a longer rehearsal time would have helped.

Finalizing

I left them to it for the next three weeks. Charmian was in the theatre most days, fitting her sessions in with the actors' schedules. It must have been very difficult for the cast, performing one version of a play while rehearsing another in parallel with it. I had never heard of such a thing being done before. Would they be able to keep the two apart in their head, during their performances, as they became more familiar with OP? I wasn't able to get up to London during those three weeks to see one of the pre-OP performances, but none of the actors afterwards reported anything untoward. It seems as if they were thinking of it as two plays.

Globe timetables are intricate things. With three productions to interweave, and two performance times during the day, matters are arranged so that, every few weeks, each of the Globe companies gets a few days off. The OP weekend had been scheduled after one of these free periods. That was good. It would give the actors time to 'forget' version A and concentrate on version B. Full rehearsals were planned for the Wednesday, Thursday and Friday before the OP weekend.

I arrived at the Globe to hear the first 'read through' on the Wednesday afternoon. I put the phrase in inverted commas because no one was actually reading anything. Having performed the play thirty-three times, they needed no script. All they had to do was

present the old lines in the new way, in character –
insofar as this was possible in the confines of a small
rehearsal room, with no movement or costume. This
time we were deep in the bowels of the theatre itself, in
a small room just off the huge Under-Globe – thought
to be the world's largest exhibition space devoted to
Shakespeare and his age.

We set the chairs in the room out in a circle, and
went through it, scene by scene. At the end of each
scene, we would stop and go over anything which
wasn't sounding right. Charmian and I made
copious notes. Both of us were very impressed. I
would say that, in aggregate, it was about 75 per
cent there. Some of the company had made more
progress than others, but everyone had entered into
the spirit of the enterprise, and the performance was
veritably zipping along. I think the actors surprised
themselves. This was the first time they had heard all
the others using OP, and during that afternoon there
was a dawning realization that, maybe, this thing was
going to work.

It was the accommodation to each other (p. 71)
that struck me most. For instance, I could hear Rhys

and Jimmy influencing each other, as they went into their Benvolio/Mercutio scene. They picked up each other's pace, and as the scene progressed so did their articulation. As one of them hit a sound with particular accuracy, so it helped the other to get there. This is exactly what I was hoping for, and it was great to hear it. Jimmy had the greater distance to travel, in this respect. Rhys was brought up in north-east Wales. Jimmy, as he describes himself, was 'a public school boy from Leicestershire'. Whereas the actors with regional roots had something they could fall back on, Jimmy had none, as his natural accent was RP – and that was precisely the accent the OP production was distancing itself from. 'I felt that using my normal voice "dried" the accent out', he told me afterwards. 'I found I needed to find some other tune to get into my OP.' And he would get that tune partly from accommodating to his friends on stage. That is how it is in real life, after all. When friends accommodate, their accents converge.

It was the same with Kananu and Tom, in their opening scene as Juliet and Romeo. To begin with there was a big distance between them. Kananu was already as accurate in OP as anyone might hope – despite a disaster earlier that week, of which more in a moment. Tom had some way to go. Their native accents were very different. Kananu's Scottish background (her name comes from a Kenyan side of the family) had given her a natural -r after vowels. Tom had none. Also, he had been trying not to overdo the -r effect, in his preparation, bearing the dangers of Mummerset in mind. But that meant there was a big gap between the pronunciations of the two leading characters. It sounded odd. There had to be more coming together. Lovers accommodate most of all.

What was exciting was to hear it happening within a few scenes. I asked Romeo at the end of the rehearsal whether he had noticed the 'pull' from Juliet. He had. It would become a focus of his work with Charmian over the next two days, and in the event the lovers emerged with a powerful linguistic rapport. This is the crucial test – not how individual actors master OP, but how their OPs meld into convincing discourse.

And Kananu's disaster? She had been assiduously working through her OP part, using a combination of tape and phonetic transcription, when –

Three days before the first performance I left all my stuff on a bus and lost them – dictaphone, tapes, phonetic script, *all*. I panicked a bit. But perhaps it was a good thing. I was forced to just listen and have a go.

An interesting point: maybe all transcriptions should have been left behind, in those last few days. (Kananu found her stuff at the Baker Street Lost Property Office – a week after the last OP performance!)

On stage

I was delighted with the way that first full rehearsal went. The problems were largely sporadic, not systematic. Several lines would go by without a hitch and then a word would catch the speaker by surprise, and a modern form would slip in. There was a fair bit of self-correction going on – prompting Tim to remind everyone not to do that when they went on stage. It was an obvious point, and hardly necessary to even mention it to such experienced actors, but worth making, as although the new accent was still in everyone's mouths, it was not yet firm in their minds. Slips of the tongue have rightly been called 'slips of the brain'. And that was the outstanding question, at the end of Wednesday. The company could talk, and they could walk, but could they do both at once?

That would emerge the next day. Thursday morning at 10, there was to be a run-through on the Globe stage. No costumes or props, but a full-speed production with entrances and exits and mock sword-fighting. Tim, Charmian, and I sat in the Lower Gallery and watched. Hilary was there too, and took a few photographs. The stage was needed at lunchtime, so it was touch-and-go whether we would get through it all. We just managed it.

The setting was rather curious. The Globe never stops. Each day it is open to visitors, and there are frequent tours of the theatre. So while the rehearsal was taking place, there would be groups of visitors arriving, sitting in the Lower Gallery for a few minutes, then moving on. It must have been a bonus for them to see something actually happening on stage. And it probably helped the actors. Several fragmentary audiences are better than no audience. A number of larger groups also passed through – children and their teacher-shepherds on school visits. And at one point I see passing in front of my eyes a friend from Stratford – Jonathan Milton, who runs the daily Shakespeare tours there. He was working with a seminar group that day. Small world.

There was no time to chat. Too much listening to do. And there was a lot to listen out for, more than the previous day. The problem was the space. In the tiny rehearsal room, the actors had no need to project. In the large outside area, they did. And what happened, of course, was that some of the carefully honed vowel qualities slipped wildly, especially in the louder and more emotional passages. As they rushed about, the OP see-sawed erratically. Kananu was a model of OP calm in a rough sea. I never heard her slip once.

Each of the actors had their own story to tell about how they felt they were coping. For Rhys Meredith (Benvolio) the problem was integration:

The most difficult thing was retaining the new pronunciations when acting. In one of the first run-throughs, I made my first entrance determined to get the accent right, and

confidently said the wrong line – then forgot my text altogether! It took a little while to take away my attention from it
and let it take care of itself. Indeed, it was not until after the
first performance that I stopped feeling self-conscious about
the sounds I was making. My occasional drift into an all too
Irish tune was a concern that stayed with me to the end and
made me wince internally every time I heard it!

For John McEnery (Friar) it brought back memories
of the scarecrow from a children's TV series, and
confronted him with the classical risk that comes
with all acting:

To see one's fellow actors morphing into Worzel
Gummidge ... the threat of corpsing was an aspect not to
be taken lightly!

We went back to the rehearsal room, and talked
about what had happened. They were all aware of
the problem, and I reckoned that at the rehearsal the
next day they would begin to allow for the setting
and get back to the level they had displayed in the
rehearsal room. And so it proved. There was only one
remaining uncertainty. What would happen when
the costumes were on? Voice coaches all know

how important it is to integrate voice work with breathing, posture, and movement in general – and all these are influenced by costume. I expected the ornate and tight-fitting costumes of the Elizabethan period to have an effect, especially on the men. I would not have been surprised to see the same blip in OP performance accuracy, when they worked in their costumes. But there could be no dress rehearsal. The schedule didn't allow it. If there was to be such a blip, we would not see it until the first night.

PR

By the time Charmian and I had got through all our notes for each character, and Tim had added his comments, it was well into lunchtime. Everyone dispersed until a final rehearsal the next day. I was expecting to be there, but events took me in a different direction. The Globe Press Office had been working assiduously trying to get some media reaction, and the day before had seen an enthusiastic piece about the production by Rupert Christiansen in the *Daily Telegraph*. Then the BBC got the message, and suddenly there was a request for interviews and recordings. I got a message from Gerry Halliday. Could I call in at the Press Office after the rehearsal? It transpired that BBC Radio News wanted to do a short item for regular transmission throughout the Friday, and the Radio 4 arts programme, *Front Row*, wanted to feature the event in their Friday evening programme. I was not surprised that an arts programme would be interested. But the News! OP was news? Well *I* thought so, of course – a once-in-400-years event is news, by any standards – but it had never crossed my mind that the BBC would agree.

As always, when the media pick up on a story, everything moves into fast forward. Both News and Radio 4 would send people round to do a recording with some of the actors. Could it be at 2 that afternoon, and could I be there to help choose the bits and add some commentary? It was already well after 1 o' clock. I had no problem, as I was staying around to take in the evening performance of *Much Ado*. But I foresaw a tiny difficulty. The BBC wanted actors. And they had all gone home.

Gerry got on the phone and started an actor-hunt. We needed just one voice for *Front Row*, but the

News wanted a snatch of dialogue – ideally, from Romeo and Juliet. However, Tom and Kananu had disappeared. They scoured the building, and found John McEnery. He could stay. A frantic phone call reached Kananu, who had just got home, and who promptly turned round and got straight back into a taxi. And so, half an hour later, in the Nancy W. Knowles Theatre, down in the basement, the BBC got their recordings. Kananu did an extract from one of her monologues, and then some dialogue with the Friar from Act 4, Scene 1. I did a short interview with the News. They had only one question really. 'How do you know?' (p. 44) And they wanted a fifteen-second sound-bite.

Front Row was a more leisurely affair – an interview at Broadcasting House the next day. Razia Iqbal was the presenter, and there was time to discuss several aspects of the production. Yes, we did the 'How do you know?', but several other points came up too. The programme went onto the Radio 4 Website afterwards. This was important: it was the first time the public could, at will, call up a piece of OP and listen to it. It is Globe practice to record all their productions for archive purposes; but these recordings stay in house. There is a full recording of one of the OP performances (25 June) as well as one of the earlier performances (10 June). They are good quality, and capture the contrast between the performances well. You have to make special arrangements to see them (p. 181).

Because of the radio recording, and some other BBC work, I missed seeing the Friday rehearsal, which was a full run-through back in the small rehearsal room. Charmian was there, and she told me it had gone very well, with a distinct improvement all round. And I must say, when I arrived in the Green Room at the end of the afternoon, there was a real air of confidence among the cast. Everyone seemed to sense it was a special occasion. Members of the other company, leaving after the afternoon *Measure for Measure* performance, wished us luck The question in everyone's mind was: how would the audience take it? The performance started at 7.30. By 10.15 we knew.

CHAPTER 5

Performance

I have never been nervous before a lecture, a broadcast, or a performance. My wife thinks I am abnormal. Personally, I think it is more to do with being in control of what is about to happen. If you have prepared properly, then what is there to be nervous about? I know many actors would disagree. Maybe I'm just lucky. But when you have prepared something for other people to perform, and you are suddenly completely out of control, that, it seems, is a different matter. As I left the Green Room before the first performance, I felt something in the pit of my stomach I did not recognize. I reported it to Hilary, and she recognized the symptoms immediately. 'Butterflies', she called them. So that's what butterflies feel like, I thought. I had only known the cast a few weeks, had hardly exchanged a hundred non-Shakespearian words with most of them, and yet I felt for them as if they were my children.

There was a real atmosphere of expectation as the audience gathered. I was curious to see who would be there. Would it be all scholars and Shakespeare buffs? No, it seemed a typical Globe audience, with an across-the-board age range, teachers and students, families, business parties, enthusiasts, Japanese tourists, Americans ... Some – as I learned in the talkback session – were unaware there was to be anything special about the performance that night until they arrived, or if they had known they had forgotten. At the same time, there was a definite presence of people who had come specifically to hear the OP. The Friends of Shakespeare's Globe were out in force. I also recognized a couple of university faces, and a few actors. There were people with an interest in Early English music. I knew a group from the Lute Society was coming on the Sunday, interested in the extent to which their musicology and my linguistics would overlap, but there were lutenists present on the Friday too.

I wandered around the yard eavesdropping on conversations. The OP was a definite talking point.

As everyone entered, the stewards gave out a bro-
chure about OP, with a foreword by Tim Carroll and
a reprint of an article on the subject I had written for
the latest issue of *Around the Globe*. They were being
avidly read. I insinuated myself into a few of the
conversations. I hadn't been imagining the sense of
expectation. People were anticipating a new theatrical experience. 'Will we understand it?' was in everyone's minds.

It was a full house. Nothing special about that,
perhaps, for most Globe performances are sold out.
Still, it was nice to know that the OP hadn't put
anyone off. On the contrary: they had been among
the earliest performances to sell out. I found myself
sitting next to a gentleman and his wife who had
travelled down from Yorkshire for the event. They
were members of a local Shakespearian society in
their home town, and, for them, this was a really
special moment. A 'once in a lifetime experience',
he said. I agreed, but thought to myself: maybe not,
in the future, if it's a success. 'Will they do it again
next year?' he asked, at the end of the evening. All I
could say was I hoped so.

I had no need to be nervous. The Friday performance was electrifying. It was so exhilarating to hear
the accent alive again, in front of an audience, for a
whole play. And there was something about the
audience. Actors can always tell when an audience
is paying real attention – as indeed, can any teacher
or lecturer. It is difficult to define, but there is something about the lack of random movement, the con-
centrated focus, which tells you – as the phrase goes –
that they are 'in your pocket'. 'Boy, but they listened',
said Jimmy Garnon, 'there was a robustness in the
listening in those shows. The air felt thicker.' It is
something which actors have a special sensitivity to,
at the Globe, with groundlings all around your feet, a
few inches away. And the consensus was that the OP
audiences were totally engaged. Several of the cast
were relieved, having heard a nasty rumour just
before the first performance went up – totally false,
but none the less worrying – that most of the audience were unaware they were attending an OP
performance in the first place. No one is immune
from anxiety when their ears are stuffed with false
reports.

The litmus test for engagement, I always think, is the kids. The Globe yard can be full of youngsters, usually school parties of secondary-school age. They can give the stewards a terrible time. Some of them are there to watch the show. Some of them are there to watch the talent. There is a lot of inattention and moving about. The actors see it all. And the most interesting comment they made to me afterwards was how this behaviour was absent, on the OP days. The kids listened too.

When I heard this, after the Friday performance, I made a point of asking some of the youngsters the next day, during the interval, how they were finding it. They knew about the OP. Their teacher had told them. So what did you think? 'Cool.' 'Wicked.' Why? One fifteen-year-old lad, in a strong south London accent, piped up. 'Well, they're talking like us.' They weren't, of course. None of the actors had anything remotely like a Cockney accent. But I knew what he meant. The actors were talking in a way that they could identify with. Had they been to other theatre shows before? Yes. And what did they think of the voices then? 'Actors always sound posh', said one.

There was a chorus of assent. 'But not here', chipped in another. RP nil, OP one.

The Friday show was the most successful one. The other two were marred, in different ways, by external circumstances. On the Sunday evening, London was blessed just before the show with some spectacular thunder and lightning, and as the performance began down came the rain. Who'd be a groundling! But everybody suffers when there is a heavy downpour, because the groundlings put on their plastic capes and hoods (available for sale in the yard) and the rain beats loudly upon them. Not the best of accompaniments for an OP performance. Still, it didn't rain for long, and most of the show was heard well enough.

It was worse on the Saturday afternoon. That was when the helicopters came. These machines are always a pain, buzzing back and forth right above the Globe, but that day they excelled themselves. It appears that the Olympic torch was being paraded around London that day, and by mid-afternoon it was due – guess where? – to cross the Millennium Bridge, right outside the theatre. For some reason two police helicopters – two! – had been assigned to keep an eye on everything. They went round and round in circles, right above our heads, drowning everything out for the best part of half-an-hour. Bette Bourne's opening speech – a joyful linguistic romp, especially in OP – was largely lost. The pilots could have watched virtually the whole of Act 1 and more, if they had wanted. It was a cruel irony, for an OP performance. I was furious. Had the police authority no soul? Had they no sense of priorities? You can see the Olympic torch every four years. This was the first time in 400. I would write to the police commissioner! I would write to the prime minister!

I would, eventually, calm down, as the torch moved away from Southwark and on towards Westminster. The helicopter noise became a distant buzz. The actors were immensely relieved. They are used to coping with Globe noises, but this had been truly exceptional. The audience relaxed, and enjoyed the rest of the show. And at the end, the applause was as long and as loud as after the other two performances. But it was a shame.

There is a point to make about the applause. Several of the cast noticed a distinct difference in the audience reaction during the OP weekend. This was not just imagination or wishful thinking. Anyone who has ever done any amateur acting knows how easy it is to judge an audience, and even quite small differences in audience response are noted and discussed afterwards. Several members of the cast told me that the end-of-show applause was more enthusiastic, and went on much longer, than on previous days. And when I compared two of the video'd performances, they were right. On 10 June, the applause did not start until half-way through the final jig (p. 153), and went on for two and a quarter minutes. On 25 June, the OP day, the applause started immediately after Escalus's closing line, and they stopped clapping three and a half minutes later.

I had three views of the show, all in the Lower Gallery. My first seat was at about 8 o'clock in rela-tion to the front of the stage – the point being that this put me on a diagonal line with one of the big pillars. Sometimes this can be a disaster for anyone sitting there, especially if the production plays too much towards the back of the stage. How to deal with the pillars is one of the big problems facing any Globe director. With this production, the only time they caused me some trouble was in the balcony scene. But – and this is the point – although my sight lines were impaired, during that scene, I was relieved to note that my hearing lines were not. Everything was very audible.

My Saturday seat was a little further round towards the centre, and my Sunday seat further round again. The sound levels stayed good. Tim was in the audience each day too – in the yard, on two occasions, moving around. The OP came across loud and clear – apart from during the helicopter moments. Interestingly, some of the phonetic effects came across more strongly than others. The short *my*'s and *thy*'s were especially distinctive, in such lines as Romeo's 'It is mi lady. O it is mi love' (2.2.10). And so were the unstressed -*y* endings sounding like 'eye' (p. 88). 'Examine other beaut*ies*', says Benvolio (1.1.228). 'Rest you merr*y*', says the Servant (1.2.62). I hadn't expected the word-endings to be so noticeable.

The OP didn't affect the humour. I have already mentioned the way Peter's joke went down well

(p. 80). In fact I didn't notice any joke being missed, because of the OP, nor could the actors recall any, when I asked them later. Perhaps more importantly, the OP didn't seem to be interfering with the specially dramatic moments, such as Juliet's 'Gallop apace' speech (3.2), Romeo's 'banished' speech (3.3), or the two monologues in the vault at the end of the play. This was where I had always located my worst fears – that the 'rustic' resonances of the accents would perhaps pull the mind away from the moment. They were groundless. Perhaps it was because the ears had attuned to the speech by then: in the talkback session, several people said they had 'got into' the OP by the end of the first couple of scenes. Or perhaps it was the impression the accent gave of being more 'down to earth' (pp. 145–8). The youngsters had made the point that they felt closer to the characters. Several adults made the same point: OP reduced the psychological distance between speaker and listener, and to that extent presented a more immediate opportunity to access the speaker's thought. For 'rustic' read 'honest', 'open', or 'direct'. Far from pulling the mind away from the moment, OP seemed to help to focus it.

Another long-term worry was what would happen to the OP when the actors donned their costumes and accoutrements. It did have some effects. Jimmy Garnon made this observation about what he was wearing:

When first I put the original practice costume on I felt myself pulled posher and camper. My RP became more pronounced and my gestures fey – which was horrible, having worked on keeping Mercutio strong and direct, and having wanted him to be someone the audience could readily relate to. I worked therefore to correct the swing. The OP in contrast suddenly made it very difficult to retain posture. It has so many rural associations in the vowels that a courtly bearing starts to feel strange. I felt myself coarsening in facial expression slightly too. RP's stiff upper lip dissolves away.

For Bette Bourne (Nurse) the problem was 'how to unify me voice with me body and me corsets'. And on the Friday night, he had one of those moments. 'Of course when I got on, I forgot everything and just had to concentrate on "What the ****" rather than the "How the ****", and try to keep the mental imagery going and keep the feeling true.' But, he added, the training had worked so well that 'it was like tramlines which kept you going along the way they'd been laid'. And gradually his inhibitions left him.

The Globe Master of Movement, Glynn MacDonald, noticed that the actors' movement became more fluent during the OP performances. And this was something Tom Cornford noticed too:

I was fascinated by the effect on the actors' bodies. Capulet's second line is a good example, where Montague 'flourishes his blade in spite of me'. In OP, *blade* sits lower and wider in the body than the RP version, and in sounding dangerous (the RP equivalent sounds very correct and polite) it makes the actor look and feel dangerous ... What OP has revealed to me is the extent to which Shakespeare's language 'bodies forth' his characters.

Interpretations

All the actors found something fresh coming out of their roles. Even if they had relatively little to say, the nature of their interaction with other characters was affected by the different rhythms and timing of the OP (p. 65). Several told me how the different pronunciation had altered their perception of their character or their behaviour during performance.

For Bette Bourne, 'The Nurse became a totally different woman ... OP toughened her up ... I didn't want her to be mumsy or soft ... She's quite ruthless to Juliet.' He found the accent helped him to be firmer with her – for example, when the Nurse has to advise her about marrying Paris. It was also a help in the gender department. 'I stopped worrying about the fact that I was a man in this role ...' The contrast between his natural pronunciation and the OP was striking: pre-OP Bette had a noticeably London accent, with glottal stops and a generally slower articulation. This disappeared during the OP performances, and his voice became distinctively more northern. He added a general comment about the experience as a whole: 'We were all suddenly "earthed" in the play. It unified us by the old sound of it; it was "a time before". That's exciting. A bit like those dramatized radio history lessons we had as kids. The same thrill ...'

A similar toughening up seemed to affect Juliet too. For Kananu Kirimi, 'Juliet felt less self-conscious and more front-footed, more aware of the company about her. She was bolder, more muscular, and that seemed to give her a greater freedom, even when alone.' She was also particularly struck by the way the OP altered her sense of the word-play within her lines. 'Juliet's word-play came to seem less intellectual and thought-based, more about pleasure than intelligence. It was more about enjoying making sounds – sounds that complicated one another, echoed one another, matched one another. As a result, I found much more humour in Juliet than I had sensed before.'

For Rhys Meredith, Benvolio was more 'driven' (p. 65):

I felt like I was going for my actions a lot more strongly. I don't think it really altered my presentation of my character, as I take the view of playwright David Mamet that there is no such thing, only yourself 'as if'. But in making me more driven in what I wanted, I certainly felt different, and the alien sounds coming from my mouth did give me a sense of otherness, especially in those moments when I was able to let it take care of itself. Listening to and speaking OP, it is 'as if' you are in a different world, which helps enormously with liberating your imagination. This drive is one of the principal things that I've tried to retain.

For Jimmy Garnon:

There is definitely something lovely in being called 'Mer-cute-io', the word 'cute' having nice connotations of brevity, cheek, wit, and studied style. It somehow made him feel more human and pulled him back away from the ideas of Mercury, magic, and mystery that the word Mercutio gives us in our modern pronunciation ... Mercutio I think felt more brilliant for the OP. The long, easy passages of wit directed at Romeo and Benvolio somehow felt more extraordinary coming out of this earthier accent.

He was particularly struck by the effect of OP on his Queen Mab speech (1.4.53). It had both pluses and minuses.

Early in rehearsals Giles Block [the Globe's Master of Words] and I were talking about the fact that the whole Mab speech is rooted in things in the revellers' immediate surroundings, in a garden at dusk or at night, and specifically for an English audience in an English rural setting – so we have hazelnuts, squirrels, grubs, spiders, grasshoppers, daddy long-legs (maybe), crickets, gnats, worms, and the moonshine's watery beams. We also have fairies. In RP this always feels like poetry. In OP suddenly it felt real. All these things seemed to come to life around me and felt like things of my world. I didn't feel I was conjuring Mab out of nothing but that she could be as real as all the other bugs. In contrast, however, as we moved into the actual world in front of me, as Mercutio suddenly looks into the audience and sees the Lovers, Courtiers, Lawyers, Soldiers, Parsons, the accent felt a burden. The rural sounds suited a rural idyll but jarred against the modern people I looked at. The satiric edge felt blunted, as the audience and I weren't speaking the same language. But overall, the accent seemed to ground Mercutio, to make him more direct and less poetic, and thus many of his attacks on the complacent felt fleshier ...

For me, all these comments were a revelation. I had never expected that such an apparently straightforward thing as a change in accent would have such dramatically (in both senses) significant consequences. I have on many an occasion, in lecturing and in print, presented a view of accent as a deep-rooted feature of human identity. I believe there is no more powerful means of expressing to others who we are and where we are from. But I had never carried the logic of this argument into the domain of dramatic characterization.

Indeed, I had been somewhat sceptical of previous attempts to bring regional accent into Shakespeare – doing a play 'in northern' or 'in Scots' or whatever.

This has been tried several times, with (according to reviews I have read) varying success. As an attempt to bring the plays closer to the people – to get rid of the distance between the kind of language most people speak and stage RP – I applauded these experiments. But I felt uncomfortable with them. To 'do' a play in a regional modern accent is to get rid of one kind of baggage, but to replace it with another. A performance of *Romeo and Juliet* in, say, a Yorkshire accent may make for a fresh intimacy as far as people from Yorkshire are concerned, but for people outside that dialect a distance nonetheless remains. Whatever cultural associations you have with the Yorkshire accent, pleasant or unpleasant, these inevitably colour your reaction to it, and it must, I felt, detract to a degree from the impact of the play. The thing about OP which makes it different from other non-RP performances – and the most fascinating thing about it is the way it occupies a unique dialect space, resonating with several modern accents and yet at a distance from all of them.

So I was delighted to find that OP had had such interesting theatrical consequences. I am unable to give them a proper interpretation and critical evaluation: that is for those involved in literary and theatre studies. All I have been able to do is record what happened, as best I can. But, as a theatregoer, the experience affected me profoundly. And it did, incidentally, make me think again about regional performances, for I am sure, now, that similarly interesting things must happen there too.

Dimensions

Regular readers of works about theatre will have noticed a certain imbalance in the present book. It has not so much been about a play as about one dimension in the production of a play; and in gathering together points of interpretation which related to that dimension, I am conscious of having said nothing about the other features which made this production of *Romeo and Juliet* memorable for me in so many other ways. I do not have the background or experience to judge the production as a whole in the manner of a theatre critic. All I can do is report my own response, and comment on what people were talking about, as I did my eavesdropping in the intervals of the three performances.

The conversation, I was glad to hear, was not only about OP. This comment should not come as a surprise. Pronunciation is, after all, only a means to an end. It must not get in the way. The play's the thing, in all its facets. In some ways, the biggest compliment that anyone could have given the OP dimension of the performance was not to feel the need to talk about it at all.

So what was the audience talking about, when they weren't talking about OP? I heard much admiration of the sumptuous, expensive, original-practice costumes – as can be seen in the photograph on the book jacket. There was much talk of the music and dance, which at the Globe is regularly more fully integrated within the action than tends to happen elsewhere. The musicians were often on stage – not, as it happens, as part of the dialogue with Peter in Act 4, Scene 5 (for that section had been cut), but in other places, sometimes unexpectedly. They stay on after the Capulets' feast, for example, when Mercutio is calling out for Romeo (2.1); and when he shouts 'Humours! Madman! Passion! Lover!' they provide appropriate instrumental responses. When Mercutio conjures Romeo by Rosaline's shape, he seizes a shapely stringed instrument from one of the musicians and traces out her curves in its form. When the Capulets are mourning Juliet's supposed death, Paris arrives with full musical accompaniment. When Romeo waits for the Apothecary to bring him poison, a band of revellers emerge from the Mantua streets and dance a devilish masque around him.

There were several places where the OP paled into insignificance, alongside some striking features of design and direction, and these were a noticeable talkback theme. In particular, when Romeo crowbars open Juliet's vault and kills Paris, the action takes place on a stone slab over the stage trapdoor. Romeo begins his final speech, and descends into the vault with Paris's body. The perspective then alters, as the stage back doors open and Juliet's tomb is wheeled into view to take its place above the stone slab, with Paris now lying at the front of it. One moment we are above the ground; the next below. It was a simple and highly effective manoeuvre, which – we may imagine – matched the ingenuity with which the original Globe actors must have used their stage.

And at the end of the play, when both are dead, lying side by side on top of the tomb, Prince Escalus speaks his final words. 'For never was a story of more woe / Than this of Juliet and her Romeo.' There is solemn music. The two bodies are lifted tenderly down and carried to the front of the stage. They are lowered to the ground, standing, facing each other. Lady Capulet joins their hands in a moment of unity. And then, in an electrifying second, the eyes of the dead couple open, they smile at each other, the music changes, and they join with the rest of the company in a joyous jig. The final jig is another Globe hallmark, but I do not recall one which has performed its emotion-releasing function quite so well.

And a last observation. The unique relationship between actor and audience at the Globe (p. 5) once again was fully exploited in some set pieces. 'Show me a mistress who is passing fair', says Romeo (1.1.234). And so Benvolio does, pointing to a female groundling. 'What if this mixture do not work at all? / Shall I be married then tomorrow morning?' asks Juliet (4.3.21). And she looks at the groundlings. 'Yes', replies one. 'No!', cries Juliet in reply. Mercutio's Mab speech, when it refers to courtiers and lawyers, is directed at the galleries – as is his later reference to 'fashion-mongers, these "pardon-me's", who stand so much on the new form that they cannot sit at ease on the old bench' (2.4.32). During the long and inventive fight scene, after an interim defeat of Tybalt, he bows to the crowd, inviting their applause, which they willingly give him.

All of this cuts across the contrast between OP and modern pronunciation. It would be wrong to exaggerate the impact of the former. It was still in essence the same production, with most of its features unaffected. And yet, having seen both versions, I am still not sure in my mind whether I have seen one play or two.

Talkback

I began to take in the implications of what had happened during the first of the two talkback sessions, on the Saturday afternoon. This is one of the benefits of having an education department in a theatre, for it allows audiences to have regular opportunities to talk about what they have experienced. They held the sessions in the Nancy W. Knowles Theatre. On both days there was a good crowd. Over seventy members of the audience stayed behind. And on the Saturday, Globe Education had assembled a really special panel.

At one end there was Mark Rylance, the Globe's artistic director. At the other, there were two of the actors, Bette Bourne and Callum Coates. In the middle was Patrick Spottiswoode, the director of Globe Education, who was acting as MC. Charmian Hoare was there. And so was Cicely Berry, the doyenne of theatrical voice for so many decades, who had watched the show that afternoon. We were all there to talk about OP. It wasn't quite the seminar we had discussed, several years before in January, but it was an intriguing line-up.

Mark began by talking generally about how the occasion had come about and how it fitted in with the Globe ethos. He introduced Tim as the most radical of his associate directors, and Tim added his perspective. I went through the 'How do we know?' exercise once again. The actors said some of the things I reported above. But we all wanted to know what Cis Berry thought. And I think we were all very relieved when she said how much she had enjoyed it. In particular, she was struck by the way the OP had invited her to explore the language anew, and to depart from previous stereotypes. It had, she said, made her listen in a different way. And she thought that an audience was ready for this kind of experiment, now. It would have been difficult when she was starting out, she said, because people were much less used to hearing dialects in public. Today, with television, they hear them all the time.

The session brought out some interesting panel and audience reactions, as people struggled to describe what it was they had heard. Charmian felt the accent had made everyone feel 'more grounded', and that the actors were 'more in touch with their bodies'. Cis was struck by the way the speech seemed to be coming more 'from within the actors'. The two actors agreed. Bette said OP 'pulled the emotions forward' – he meant that he felt greater prominence was being given to the jaw, which is indeed a feeling which comes from using longer, tenser vowels. The rural resonances added a 'simple sincerity', said Tim. Callum thought it 'brought vitality and removed pomposity'. Bette capped them all, for metaphor. OP, he said, 'had the sound of brown ale'.

I was pleased to see that the talkback sessions weren't all mutual chin-stroking. There were criticisms to be made too. Charmian pointed out she had had to make compromises, when working with the cast. Some had found the exercise quite difficult, and with very limited rehearsal time she had been unable to achieve the level of consistency she wanted. This was fair comment. Even in the third performance, I was noticing words which were still some way from the OP target. And both Callum and Bette felt that another week was needed before that kind of problem could be eliminated.

At the end, I asked the assembly whether they would like to see the OP experiment repeated. There was a resounding and unanimous 'YES'. Mark was impressed, by both the accessibility of the performance and the enthusiasm of the audience.

He was not averse, he intimated, to the OP run continuing – but only if there was unanimity among the
actors. If everyone wanted it, the Globe would let it
happen. In the end, that unanimity was lacking. I do
not know who was against the idea, and I did not ask.
At the time, I regretted the decision, but I think
perhaps it was the right one. Audiences later in the
season might have been uncomfortably surprised by
the change. And what would have been a significant
theatrical event – a whole season in OP – would have
received less critical attention than it deserved. As it
was, the critics, as far as I know, totally ignored the
weekend. It was such a pity. I would love to have read
what some of the well-known writers thought about it.
Another time, maybe.

The talkback session on the Sunday, after the evening performance, didn't start until around 9.30, so it
wasn't as full. This time Tom Cornford came up
front, along with Patrick, Charmian, Callum, and
myself, and Tim sat in the audience. It was a very
similar occasion to the previous day, in terms of the
questions asked and the comments made. The point
about accent awareness prompted a great deal of

discussion, this time within a global perspective. It is a perspective which can be perceived in contemporary London, home today to over 300 languages. With widespread immigration, London has become a melting-pot of accents again – just as it was in early modern England.

However, one question was different. A member of the audience, a Shakespeare teacher, said she was going to introduce the topic of OP into her course next academic session, and where could she read up about it? In particular, was I going to write up the story of the OP weekend at the Globe, to include the various points which had come up in the talkback? It hadn't occurred to me, I must say. But as soon as she mentioned it, I saw the point, and this book was born.

The session ended, and the audience drifted away. It was getting on for midnight. Patrick walked Ben and I back through the theatre, deserted now apart from the security men. The stage-door exit was locked, at that time of night, so he let us out through an unfamiliar side door, and we said farewell. We found ourselves in the almost deserted car park.

Normally crammed with vehicles, my car was the only one still there. There was rain still in the air, and a wind coming off the Thames. It suddenly felt very lonely. As I got in, I saw Callum sitting outside the actors' shack, talking to a friend. 'Good night', I said in OP. 'Good night', he echoed. And it was over.

CHAPTER 6

Consequences

Well, almost over . . . I was driving back to Holyhead
the next day when the mobile phone rang. It was a
message from the Globe asking me to ring the
Richard and Judy show. They were interested in
doing a piece on OP. Was I in London? Well no,
actually, Hilary told the researcher. We are on the M6
heading north-west. Could we be in London tomorrow? Not possible . . . meetings at home already
planned. What about Wednesday?

Richard and Judy is a UK television chat-show that
has made something of a mark for itself in recent
times – an hour-long programme airing daily at 5
o'clock in the afternoon. It is produced in London by
CactusTV for Channel 4, and in 2004 was attracting
an audience approaching 3 million. It has a reputation for dealing with serious topics in an intelli-
gent way. If I wanted the OP project to come to the

attention of a large number of people, this was a proposal I could hardly ignore! And I was impressed that a popular programme like this should have shown an interest.

That is why I found myself on a train from Holyhead to London on the Wednesday morning. Not the best day to be in London, as it happened. There was a 24-hour tube strike. But if anything, the traffic was lighter between Euston and the CactusTV studios, just round the corner from the Oval cricket ground on the South Bank, and I arrived in good time.

The day before I had had a couple of conversations with Anne Stone, the researcher assigned to the item, and we had worked out how to proceed. They were going to film Kananu and Tom doing a piece of the dialogue for the balcony scene, and they were proposing to show this in contrast with an extract from the same scene from *Shakespeare in Love*, starring Gwyneth Paltrow and Joseph Fiennes. It was a brilliant idea. Seeing the two versions side by side made the contrast between RP and OP stand out more clearly than any amount of linguistic description could have achieved. The chat lasted only about six minutes, but it covered a lot of ground. As ever, old faithful 'How do you know?' was the front-running question.

It never ceases to amaze me how many people listen to the radio, still, these days, despite TV and Internet distractions. But I am absolutely staggered by what happens when you talk about a topic on television. Suddenly, the world and its dog seems to know about it. CactusTV feedback received many positive viewer reactions. And I received calls and emails from all over. Not all were displaying a merely transient interest. Two were organizations interested in hearing more, via the lecture-circuit. And an amateur repertory company wondered whether it would be possible to do the same thing themselves. The OP ripples, it seems, were spreading.

The Internet began to spread them further. On the Saturday of the OP weekend, someone posted a message on the US-moderated Shakespeare forum, www.shaksper.net, asking whether anyone had been to see the production. Somebody had, and within a couple of days there was a flurry of postings from interested Shakespearians in various parts of the world. I answered some of the questions that were coming up, and as a result made some valuable contacts. Several would prove to be long-term.

Theatrical

The media interest died away, and I settled down to this book. But even as I began to write it, I knew the story was not entirely over. I could write Chapter 1, but not yet Chapter 6. There was an outstanding question. Would the actors be able to revert to modern pronunciation with ease, once they had left the weekend behind?

They had four free days in which to get over it, and discover their other voices again. I suspected that they would find it difficult to wean themselves away, and so did Tim Carroll. We were right. Rhys Meredith takes up the story:

The very first performance after we reverted to modern pronunciation the first actual line of text to come out of anybody's mouth was Tas with his 'Do you bite your thumb?' – which from where most of the cast were standing backstage sounded distinctly OP. When I mentioned it to him afterwards, he said 'I hoped nobody noticed.' More remarkable, as it was quite a few performances later, was Joel's first speech as Escalus. For one performance only, it took on rather a Devon sound – much to my amusement as I stood there being reprimanded by him!

This see-sawing was only to be expected. But I wondered how long it would last. I had booked in to see the show again three weeks later, precisely for that reason. Would there be any sign of OP then?

There was. The pace seemed to have been retained. There were many shortened grammatical words (p. 62), and individual pronunciations were still occasionally coming through. Bill Stewart, who played Capulet in an energetic, clipped style, was so enamoured of the staccato rhythm resulting from sequences of shortened forms that he retained several of them in his later performances – 'mi hearts ... mi house'. I also heard the extra syllable in word-endings a number of times – 'substant-i-al', 'lamenta-ti-on', 'infec-ti-on', 'mar-i-age' ... And the resonance of Kananu's Scottish -r after vowels was a permanent reminder of what had been.

None of the accent-mixing, I imagine, would have been noticed by any of the audience, unless it contained a stray phonetician. Most listeners would probably have put it down to the accent diversity which was a feature of the cast, and which Tim Carroll had from the outset been privileging in his approach to the play. Certainly the actors' natural voices were varied in their own right, representing several parts of the country. In this respect, the OP ethos was maintained – and, indeed, had been there right from the start.

Most members of the company seemed to have regrets about returning to a modern sound. They had, after all, come on quite a journey from those early moments of suspicion and panic (p. 110) to a position of ownership and confident exploitation. 'I found it quite difficult going back to RP, when the three shows were done', said Bette Bourne. 'It seemed suddenly a bit prissy. We'd gone back to the modern sense of class.' Joel Trill commented: 'when we went back to RP it felt a little fraudulent, after experiencing something as earthy and resonant as OP, and I found myself keeping certain sounds, such as the [eː] in words like *peace*.' Some had fallen in love with particular words or lines, and were sad to lose them. Kananu

Kirimi had become enamoured of _comfortable_, with two stresses, which she uses in her final scene: it reminded her of 'come for Tybalt'. Rhys Meredith remarked: 'One of the things I most miss is saying "Here comes the Capulets" in OP. It always conjured up the image of them being some sort of Spanish band!'

Whatever their final feelings about the experiment, all the actors were aware, I think, that they had participated in something rather special. In the final round of correspondence, which generated the messages from the cast which I have been quoting throughout the book, there was repeated reference to the process of discovery – how OP had helped them to get closer to the metre, how it helped them find fresh phonetic echoes and rhymes within and between lines. And there was a more general legacy too. Here is Charmian's final comment:

I love the idea that there were many acceptable ways of pronouncing the language, as often I find myself working with directors who insist on certain pronunciations and methods of 'speaking' Shakespeare. I found the OP perspective very liberating. I also loved the way that it 'rooted' the language and gave it a 'gutsy' and 'earthy' quality. For me it has taken some of the 'mystique' away from Shakespeare, and made his language much more accessible and less precious. I found the whole project very exciting. It really opened up a whole new way of looking at Shakespeare, and I can't read now without the OP ringing in my head!

And this from one of the cast (Rhys Meredith):

The experiment as a whole was fascinating and I think that it has probably been of enormous benefit, not only for the show as a whole, but in terms of my playing Shakespeare in the future. It is the colloquial aspect of the OP that I think will stick with me the most. I have always felt that Shakespeare should be spoken as real people speak, as Hamlet says and as Tim has repeatedly stressed, and I think that bearing in mind the fluidity of OP even when not doing it in OP is a real stride forward in reclaiming Shakespeare from a precious and over-reverent attitude.

And this from another (Jimmy Garnon):

I think many people have an inappropriate prejudice against rural sounds. To present a careless genius like Mercutio speaking in that way, to remind people that Shakespeare may have spoken in that way, can only be a good thing.

'It was a wonderful experiment', reflected Joel Trill. No member of the cast disagreed.

Future

As scientists say, the important thing about experiments is that they are replicable. The Globe had originally decided on only a three-day run because they had no idea whether the experiment was going to be successful. Perhaps the audience would not understand the actors? Perhaps they *would* understand them, but find the unfamiliar accent unacceptable? With no precedents to refer to, there must have been lots of hypothetical worries on the table when the management first met to talk about it, and I can quite understand that they would have wanted to dip a very cautious toe in the water.

In the event, as I now know, the worries were groundless, and the overall tone of the talkbacks and subsequent conversations was positive and forward-looking. There were several murmurs about doing the thing again, but properly this time, with an OP production carried through a whole season. I hope they do it. This would give the accent a real chance to show its colours, give the company the time they needed to eliminate inconsistencies, and allow them the chance to explore its potential as a medium of expression to the full.

If I were involved in another such production, would I do anything differently? Most certainly. I think I would structure my opening session afresh, now that I know so much more about the actors' feelings and expectations. I would keep the transcription as it is, but I would add extra teaching aids. Several excellent ideas arose from the actors in the course of the work which would be well worth incorporating. One was the importance of focusing on the most distinctive words. Rhys found this important, in learning his part: 'as long as I held on to the really unusual words and headed for them, then I began to produce something that sounded different'. Bill had found it useful to go through the text he had used when learning his part originally, highlighting the words which were different. Bette thought a small dictionary of the least familiar words would have been helpful – making me think again about the value of the third approach to transcription that I had presented to Tim and Tom in January (p. 39). I would do all this, if there was a next time.

I still think the idea of a seminar is a good one. We must not forget that my transcription is a beginning, not an end. It would be a disaster if it were taken as some sort of standard and copied slavishly. The decisions I have made need critical evaluation, and alternative choices need to be part of further experiments. A thoroughgoing debate about where we are at, in Early Modern English phonology, would be a very good thing.

And why stop with Early Modern English? If an original accent works for Shakespeare, why not for other dramatists and for other periods. I have heard Chaucer in OP. What about the Restoration dramatists? Or more recent ones? It has always struck me as curious that a play from the eighteenth or nineteenth centuries is faithfully presented using its dialect grammar and vocabulary, because this is reflected in the text, but its associated pronunciation is not, because it is hidden by the standard English spelling. Why not Sheridan in OP? Or, for that matter, Oscar Wilde?

'Almost over', I said at the beginning of this chapter. I am beginning to realize that this experiment may never be over.

EPILOGUE

One other thing happened during the OP weekend. At the very end, on the last night. I was sitting on my bench, enjoying the jig, when I noticed Tim Carroll in the yard trying to catch my eye. He gestured me to come down. We had a talkback session to do immediately afterwards, so I thought he wanted us to get down to the Nancy Knowles before the crowd. But when I joined him he just stood there. We watched the jig come to an end, and then, Melanie Jessop (Lady Capulet) came to the front of the stage and asked for silence. What on earth was going on? I had to rely on Ben, who was in the audience with me that night, to tell me afterwards what exactly happened, because it blew my recall memory clean out of my head.

She thanked the audience and told everyone what a marvellous weekend it had been. There was a cheer.

Then I was startled to hear my own name and my role described. I looked at Tim aghast. He was grinning. There was another cheer. 'Where are you, David?' called Mel. I gave a weak wave. And she called me up. I walked to the front of the yard. The audience had erupted into applause. Do you know how high that stage is? Over five foot. My chin reached it. All I could do was raise my arms and pray. I was hauled up, unceremoniously, by I forget who – I think the Friar may have been part of it. I found myself on stage, with a company I had grown to love. I looked at them all. They seemed thrilled to bits. Jimmy told me later: 'to haul a bearded academic in jacket and tie up onto a theatre stage and to hear him so loudly and hotly applauded is a memory that will stay with me for a very long time'. And me. There was a final bow, and we walked off together. I got a kiss from Juliet. For an aging historical linguist, that is as good as it gets.

APPENDIX 1

Chief distinctive Early Modern English vowels

	Modern English	EME	Examples
1	ʌ	ɤ	love, blood, grudge
2	iː	eː	scene, unclean, meet
3	ɑː	aː	marked, star, father
4	eɪ	eː[1]	say, rage, take, break
5	aɪ	əɪ	lie, life, strive, alike
6	ɔɪ	əɪ	toy, loins, toil
7	əʊ	oː	both, foes, go, overthrows
8	aʊ	əʊ	now, our, house
9	ɪə	iː	hear, ears, here, fear
10	ɛə	ɛː	fair, pair, their, where
11	aʊə	oː	hour, flowers

[1] More open than the vowel in 'scene', etc.

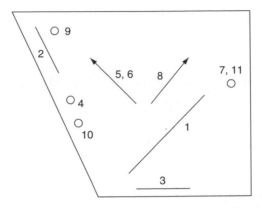

The range of pronunciation thought to be associated with the vowels in the table on p. 175, shown using the Cardinal Vowel Diagram representation of the vowel area in the centre of the mouth. The movement of the tongue in the diphthongs is shown by arrows.

Extracts from the transcription

These extracts provide a fuller illustration of the transcription described in Chapter 3. Capulet illustrates some of the more conservative choices discussed there.

From the beginning of Act I, Scene 2:

CAPULET

1   But Montague is bəʊnd as well as əɪ,

2   In penaltəɪ aləɪke; ən tis nat haːɹd, ə think,

3   Fəɹ men so: oːld as we: tə keːp the peːce.

PARIS

4   Of hᴜnᴏᴜɹəble recknin aːɹə yə boːth,

5   ən pitəɪ tis yə lived ət odds sə long.

6   But nəʊ, mɪ loːɹd, hwɑt se: yə tə mɪ syuit?

CAPULET

7   But se:yin oːɹ hwɑt əɹ əv said bɪfoːɹː

8   Mɪ chəɪld is yɪt a streːngeɹ in the wɑɹld;

9   Shɪ ath nat seːn the cheːnge ə foːɹteːn yeːɹs,

10   Let two moːɹ sʏməɹs witheɹ in thəɹ prəɪde,

11   ɛːɹ weː meː think əɹ rəɪpe tə beː a brəɪde.

PARIS

12   Yʏngeɹ than she əɹ happəɪ mʏtheɹs meːde.

CAPULET

13   ən too soon maːɹed əɹ thoːse soː eaɹləɹ meːde.

14   eaːɹth əth swællowed[a] aːll mɪ hoːpes but sheː;

15   Shɪz the hoːpeful leːdəɹ of mɪ eaɹth.

16   But woo əɹ, gentle Paɹis, get əɹ haːɹt.

17   Mɪ will tə heɹ consent is but a paːɹt,

18   This nəɪght ə hoːld an oːld accʏstomed fest,

19   Wheːɹeto əɪ ave invəɪted mænəɹ[a] a gest,

20   Sʏch as əɪ lʏve; ən you amʏng the stoːɹe,

21   Oːn moːɹe, moːs welcome, meːkes mɪ nʏmbeɹ moːɹe.

22   ət məɪ poːɹ həʊse look to bɪhoːld this nəɪght

23   Eaɹth-treadin staːɹs that meːk daːɹk heaven ləɪght.

From the middle of Act 1, Scene 4:

ROMEO

50.1   ə dreamt a dream tənəɪght.

MERCUTIO

50.2   ən soː did əɪ.

ROMEO

51.1   Well, hwɑt wɑs yuːɹs?

MERCUTIO

51.2   That dreameɹs ɒftən ləɪ.

ROMEO

52   In bed asleep, hwəɪle theːy do dream things true.

MERCUTIO

53   Oː, then ə see Queen Mab əth been with you.

54   She is the fɛːɹəɪs' midwəɪfe, ən shɪ cʊms

55   In sheːpe noː biggeɹ than an agɪt stoːne

56   On the foːɹefingeɹ əv ən ældeɹmɑn,ᵃ

57   Drawn with a team ə little atoməɪs

58   Oːɹ men's noːses əz theːy ləɪ asleep.

59   əɹ chaɹyot is an emtəɪ heːzelnʊt

60   Meːd bɪ the jəɪneɹ skiɹel or oːld grʊb,

179

61 Təɪme əʊt ə məɪnd the fɛːɹəɪs' coːchmeːkeɹs.

62 əɹ wagon spoːkes meːd ə long spinneɹs' legs;

63 The cɤveɹ, of the wings of graːsshoppeɹs;

64 əɹ treːces, of the smaːllest spəɪdeɹ web;

65 əɹ collaɹs, of the moonshəɪne's wɑːtɹəɪ beams;

66 əɹ hwip, of cricket's boːne; the lash, of filəm;

67 əɹ wagoneɹ, a smaːll greːy-coːated gnat,

68 Not haːlf sə big as a rəʊnd little wɑːɹm

69 Pricked from the leːzəɪ fingeɹ of a meːd.

70 ənd in this steːte shɪ gallops nəɪght bɪ nəɪght

71 Through lɤveɹs' breːns, ən then theːy dream ə lɤve;

72 Oːɹ coːɹtɪeɹs' knees, that dream on coːɹtsəɪs streːght;

73 Oːɹ loːweɹs' fingeɹs, who streːght dream on fees;

74 Oːɹ leːdies' lips, who streːght on kisses dream,

75 Hwich oft the angrəɪ Mab with blisteɹs pleːgues,

76 Because thɛːɹ breaths with sweetmeats teːnted aːɹe.

ᵃ The [æ] symbol was used to remind the actors to avoid the modern pronunciations of the *a* spelling in these words.

Audio-visual aids

A reading of some extracts from the play, along with the transcription, can be accessed at www.shakespeareswords.com

Videos were made of two performances of the play, for 10 June (in modern pronunciation, twenty-eight performances into the run) and for 25 June (the opening OP performance). These are available for viewing in-house at the Globe by appointment. Viewing arrangements can be made via the Globe Research Library Staff.

Shakespeare's Globe
21 New Globe Walk
Bankside
London SE1 9DT
Tel +44 (0)20 7902 1400
Fax +44 (0)20 7902 1401
www.shakespeares-globe.org

INDEX

The alphabetical arrangement of the index is letter-by-letter.

accent of the age 27
accents
    actors using their own 24–5, 27, 111,
        113, 118, 166
    identity function of 148
    mixed 164–7
    modern regional 21, 23, 89, 91–3, 148–9
    standard 27, 80–1
    see also Early Modern English
accommodation 26, 71, 121–3
actors
    reaction to OP 143–8, 164–7
    teaching IPA to 31–2
age and accent 41, 72–5
Anglo-Saxon spelling 46
announcement before the play 105–6
apostrophes 48, 60–1
applause 139–40
a pronunciations 83
Armin, Robert 26
Around the Globe 11, 135
As You Like It 41
audiences
    expectations of 113
    Globe 5–6, 92–3, 134–6, 153–4
    Romeo and Juliet 7, 113, 126, 150–4

audio-teaching 32–3
auditions 27, 41
authenticity 7

Barber, Charles 19
Barton, John xi–xii, 10, 15, 20, 33, 58,
    101, 113
BBC 128–30
Benvolio, character of 146
Berry, Cicely 155–6
'best' speech 26
Block, Giles 147
boredom 33
Boundy, Neville 57
Bourne, Bette 69, 101, 102, 114, 139, 143,
    145, 155–7, 170
Burke, Tom 101, 108, 122–3, 130, 162

Callan, Debs xvii, 11, 13–17, 58
*Cambridge History of the English
    Language, The* 20
Carroll, Tim xv, 8, 16, 17, 27, 34, 36,
    40–1, 56, 58, 64, 69, 76, 97–8, 103,
    109–10, 112–13, 124–5, 128, 135, 141,
    155–8, 164, 166, 170, 173–4
characterization 22

character scripts 97–8
Charlton, Sid xvii, 97, 104
Chaucer, Geoffrey 73, 171
child language 119
Christiansen, Rupert 128
class differences 22, 41, 63, 66, 69, 71, 111
Coates, Callum 101, 155, 157, 160
Cockney 66, 137
colloquial style 61–3, 70–1, 168
common core 76–88
Condell, Henry 26
Connolly, John Paul 101, 105
consonants
    Early Modern English 79–82
    omission of 61–2
Cornford, Tom xvii, 16–17, 21, 36,
        56, 59, 64, 97–9, 104, 107, 144,
        158, 170
'correct' pronunciation 67
costumes 151
    effect of 127–8, 143
Crystal, Ben 12, 31, 57, 159, 173–4
Crystal, David xvii
Crystal, Hilary 57, 125
cue-scripts 97
cuts 57, 105, 107

dance 151
dialect coaches 28, 35, 58, 59, 94
diphthongs 82, 86–9
director decisions 152–3
    OP influencing 21–2, 76, 81, 112
Dobson, E. J. 19, 54
Dodsley, Robert 43
Dogberry 17
dog's letter 50–1
Doran, Gregory 57
dramaturgy 40–1, 112, 148–50

Drake, Francis 26
dual alphabet 59–60

Early Modern English 12, 28, 171
    American history of 93–4
    changes in 72–4
    range of accents in 25–7, 60–75
    vowel system of 175
    see also original pronunciation
ear-training 31
educated speech 63, 67–71
elision 48, 60–2, 70
Elizabethan actors 26–7
Elyot, Thomas 67–8
Emiabata, Tas 101, 106, 164
emotional speech 69–70, 119, 126

'far back' 84–5
Fiennes, Joseph 162
findout.tv 18
First Folio spellings 47, 70
formality 60–1
Fowler, Henry 67
Friends of Shakespeare's Globe 134
Front Row 129–30

Garnon, Jimmy 23–4, 28, 65, 101, 110,
        118, 122, 136, 143, 147, 168, 174
g-dropping 22, 47, 70–1, 79, 115
Gimson, A. C. 19, 21
Globe see Shakespeare's Globe
Globe Education 11, 12, 43–4, 155
Globe Playhouse Trust 2
Globe practitioners 44
grammatical words 62–4, 66,
        141, 165
groundlings 5–6, 136, 138, 153–4
Guthrie, Tyrone 20

half-rhyme 52
Hall, Peter 20, 44, 59
Halliday, Gerry 129
Hamlet 6, 13
Hart, John 49
h-dropping 65–9, 79
helicopters 6
Heminge, John 26
Henry V 3, 5–6
Hoare, Charmian xvii, 98–9,
    100, 108–9, 112, 114–19, 121,
    123, 125, 128, 131, 155–6,
    158, 167
Holofernes 48–9, 66–8
homophones 87
humour 80, 141, 146
hypercorrection 22–3

iambic metre 77–8
identity and accent 148
imitating accents 33–4
inconsistency 119
individual word pronunciations
    89–90
International Phonetic Alphabet 25,
    29–31
Internet forum 163–4
intonation 13, 113
Iqbal, Razia 130

James I, King 26
Jessop, Melanie 101, 173
jigs 153, 173
Johnson, Samuel 43
Jones, Daniel 21, 34
Jonson, Ben 49–50
Juliet, character of 145
Julius Caesar 10, 20

Kirimi, Kananu 64, 92, 101, 108, 122–4,
    126, 130, 145–6, 162, 165, 167
Kökeritz, Helge 19, 54, 105

language change 46–7, 72, 87, 113
Lass, Roger 20
Latin 50
Linguaphone 31
liquid sounds 50
'little' words 61–4
London accents 25–6, 159
loudness of speech 126
Love's Labour's Lost 48, 66

Macbeth 93
MacDonald, Glynn 144
McEnery, John 101, 127, 130
McGinity, Terry 101
Mamet, David 146
Marlowe Society 20
Marsen, Julie 101
Master of Movement 144
Master of Voice 35
Master of Words 147
Measure for Measure 131
Mercutio, character of 147–8
Meredith, Rhys 24, 64, 101, 102, 110, 111,
    117–18, 121, 126, 146, 164–5, 167,
    168, 170
metre 48, 51, 77–8
Milton, Jonathan 120
Much Ado About Nothing 99, 129
Müller, Simon 101, 118
music 134, 151–2
myths about Elizabethan English 93–4

Nancy W. Knowles Theatre 130,
    155, 173

New Penguin Shakespeare 56
Newton, Robert 23
Nightingale, Florence 46
non-segmental pronunciation 13, 113
non-standard pronunciations 63
Nurse, character of 69, 145

OP *see* original pronunciation
original practices 7–8, 143, 151
original pronunciation
  alternative versions of 53
  books on 19
  changes in 41, 72
  character of 91–3, 113, 142–3, 149,
    167–8
  common core of 76–88
  deciding to do 8–9
  decisions about transcription
    55–60
  evidence of 45–54, 156, 163
  informality of 62
  intelligibility of 36–7, 135, 157–8, 169
  Internet discussion of 163–4
  long-term effect of 164–7
  modern accents compared to 21–2,
    37, 91–3
  presenting other authors in 171
  television discussion of 161–3
  uncertainty about 13, 52–3
  uniqueness of 149
  variation in 25–7, 41, 60–75, 77–81
orthoepists 49–51, 67–9, 76, 80
Othello xi, 57
owning the accent 116–17

Paltrow, Gwyneth 162
Patterson, Brian 105, 109
Penguin *Factfinder* 18

phonetics, historical 14
phonetic transcription 12–13, 29–32, 56
  full vs partial 37–9, 59–60
phonology, historical 14
Playing Shakespeare 20
pronouns 63–4
puns 41, 51, 54, 70, 73, 77, 87

Quarto spellings 80, 90
Queen Mab speech 147–8

-*r* after vowels 22, 24, 50, 79, 80–1,
    112, 123
Raleigh, Walter 26
Received Pronunciation 26–7, 80–5,
    122, 143, 147, 149, 162, 166
  affected 82
recordings
  Globe 131, 181
  Radio 4 130
regional performances 149–50
rehearsals 97–131, 157
re-spelling 30
rhymes 51–4, 66, 77, 167
rhythms 51, 77–8, 113
Richard and Judy 55, 161–3
Robeson, Paul xi
Robins, Nick 11
Rodenburg, Patsy 61
Romeo and Juliet
  character interpretations in 144–8
  cuts in 57
  duration of 65
  effect of helicopters on 138–9
  effect of rain on 138
  OP performances 133–60
  parallel performances of 120
  post-OP performances of 164–7

production features of 150–4
video of 140, 181
RP *see* Received Pronunciation
rustic impression 22, 81, 142, 157
Rylance, Mark xvii, 6, 10, 100,
    155, 157

schwa 62
segmental pronunciation 13
self-correction 124
seminar on OP 11, 13–17, 41, 56, 58,
    155, 171
Shakespeare in Love 162
Shakespeare's accent 26
Shakespeare's Globe
    audience involvement in 5–6
    history of 1–2
    Library at 181
    open-air character of 6–7
    Press Office at 128–9
    reconstruction of 2–4
    schedules for 120
    seating at 140–1
    tours of 125
Shakespeare's Words 12
    website for 18–19, 181
shaksper site 163–4
silent letters 68
Smith, Captain John 93
sociolinguistics 69, 71
sound patterns 51–4
speed of speech 60–1, 65, 112–13
spelling
    influencing pronunciation 48, 66–7
    representing speech 54, 61–3, 80
    used as evidence 46–9
Spottiswoode, Patrick 43, 45, 155,
    158, 159

standard English 63
stereotyped accents 22–3, 156
Stewart, Bill 70, 101,
    165, 170
Stone, Anne 162
stress patterns 64, 66
Story of English, The 20
styles 60–76
Swan theatre 3
systemic transcription 39–40

talkback sessions 58, 92–3, 100,
    142, 152, 154–9, 173
tape recording
    provided 99, 104, 107–9, 117
    rejected 31–2
Tempest, The 5, 7
Theatre playhouse 3
transcription
    actors not to be shown 104
    arguments for and against 29–35
    completion of 94–5
    extracts of 177–80
    future modifications to 170
    proposal for 15, 17
    types of 37–40, 59, 170
Trill, Joel 92, 101, 118, 165,
    166, 168
trilled sounds 50
tripping pronunciation 13, 49, 61
Twelfth Night 8
Two Gentlemen of Verona, The 2

Under-Globe 121
uneducated speech 63
uniformity, phonetic 25
unison speech 114
University of Wales, Bangor 18

voice coaches 35, 128
vowels
   centralized 22, 83, 87
   difficult 115, 117–18
   Early Modern English 82–9, 175–6
   long 84–6
   omission of 61
   pure 89
   short 82–4
   short vs long 82
   spoken and written 54–5

Walker-Brown, Rowan xvii
Wanamaker, Sam xi, 2, 12, 45
Wells, John 94
West Country accent 23
wh-, pronunciation of 40, 79, 115
Williamisms 12
women's speech 69
word-play 87–8, 146
Wordplay 12

young people's reaction 137–8, 142